The Nature of Science

The Nature of Science

*Integrating Historical, Philosophical,
and Sociological Perspectives*

Fernando Espinoza

ROWMAN & LITTLEFIELD PUBLISHERS, INC.
Lanham • Boulder • New York • Toronto • Plymouth, UK

Published by Rowman & Littlefield Publishers, Inc.
A wholly owned subsidary of The Rowman & Littlefield Publishing Group, Inc.
4501 Forbes Boulevard, Suite 200, Lanham, Maryland 20706
http://www.rowmanlittlefield.com

Estover Road, Plymouth PL6 7PY, United Kingdom

British Library Cataloguing in Publication Information Available

Library of Congress Cataloging-in-Publication Data

Espinoza, Fernando.
  The nature of science : integrating historical, philosophical, and sociological perspectives / Fernando Espinoza.
      p. cm.
  Includes bibliographical references and index.
  ISBN 978-1-4422-0951-0 (hardback) — ISBN 978-1-4422-0952-7 (paper) — ISBN 978-1-4422-0953-4 (electronic)
  1. Science—Study and teaching—Philosophy. 2. Science—Social aspects. I. Title.
  Q181.E695 2011
  507.1—dc23
                                                        2011015776

∞™ The paper used in this publication meets the minimum requirements of American National Standard for Information Sciences—Permanence of Paper for Printed Library Materials, ANSI/NISO Z39.48-1992.

Printed in the United States of America

Contents

Preface

This book is the result of years of reflection on what should be the most important features of science that students ought to know to be prepared for work in any scientific discipline. It is important to remember that science, by definition, is a body of knowledge that increases at a pace which makes it virtually impossible for anyone to fully master. Nevertheless, it is important for citizens to know *how* it is used, and for what purposes.

The dominant role that science and scientific knowledge have come to play in the modern world can be intimidating, often predisposing the nonscientific population to a self-imposed view of science that is inherently problematic given its overwhelming impact on modern life. For this reason, several excellent attempts have been made to facilitate the way scientific discoveries and their applications are communicated to the public.[1] The overarching principle of these attempts has been the development of scientific literacy among the general population. However, the emphasis has been to a large extent on the clarification and provision of factual information that is felt to be needed for the development of such literacy.[2] This approach has been found wanting by national scientific organizations concerned with the development of scientific literacy; their conclusion has been that an understanding of the *practices* of science and engineering is as important as the acquisition of knowledge of its content.

The information considered relevant to the development of scientific literacy has been structured as either that resulting from recent scientific discoveries and their applications or that needed by the population to make well-informed decisions. A particular limitation of these approaches is that they treat information in a way that confirms what the intended audience has already come to regard science as being—that is to say, they enhance the perception that, to be well informed, one must regard scientific knowledge as the most authoritative source of information there can possibly be.

The approach to be followed in this book is more comprehensive and holistic: Science is to be seen as a general *type* of knowledge with distinctive characteristics that shares many human traits found in other forms of knowledge. A broader sort of background knowledge is needed for students to be able to comprehend and, more importantly, to apply the concepts that constitute such a generalized form of scientific literacy. To accomplish this, it is necessary to deal with science's origins and development, as well as with its practice. To this extent, one must first deal with the historical and philosophical aspects of scientific knowledge and then address the sociological aspects that are the inevitable consequence of its applications. Therefore, the first few chapters contain a survey of the development of knowledge about the natural world that is necessary for a comprehensive view of how science originated.

Chapter 1 sets the stage for the discussion by conveying to the reader that scientific literacy has become a modern professional imperative, thereby requiring an understanding of the impact of scientific knowledge on most aspects of life. The particular view of progress that has resulted from dominion over nature has definite implications for a sociological perspective on what science can legitimately do and what it cannot do.

Chapter 2 offers a chronological summary that includes certain prehistoric and ancient events, which is necessary to provide a larger perspective for the reader to see that scientific knowledge has evolved from views that preceded the seventeenth century. Many treatises on scientific knowledge usually begin with that century as the "officially" accepted beginning of science, but this approach gives the audience a rather naive impression that humanity suddenly awakened then from previous ignorance, thus failing to acknowledge the many questions about nature that had been entertained before modern science emerged and that continue to be debated. In other words, a historical perspective that begins with the seventeenth century is indeed narrow-minded. The chapter ends with a chart of the flow of knowledge that truly encompasses such a perspective by showing how different cultures have influenced and continue to influence one another.

Chapter 3 deals with the earliest comprehensive and rationalistic syntheses. The general significance of Greek contributions to knowledge forms the bulk of this chapter; the presentation is divided into the pre-Socratic period, the period of Plato and Aristotle, and the Hellenic/Hellenistic period. The goal is to demonstrate the evolution of the earliest attempts to provide a comprehensive view of nature, which is after all the goal of science. A short discussion of some general philosophical definitions is therefore unavoidable in the context of a consideration of different forms of knowledge.

Chapter 4 consists of a discussion of the Greek legacy as it manifested itself in two examples: first, its influence on Roman knowledge in general, with a particular emphasis on engineering and architecture as examples of the practicality of scientific knowledge, even if not technically defined as such during that period; second, the Arab contributions to medieval knowledge, which were absolutely essential to the emergence of science as a distinct way to look at nature.

Chapter 5 is one of the central chapters of the book, in which the scholastic period is used as an example of the harmony that can exist between the spiritual and the material accounts of reality. The beginnings of empiricism and the use of inductive knowledge to investigate nature are illustrated. One of the main objectives is to show the reader that the use of logic led medieval Europe to adopt a perspective on nature that became irreversible and that inexorably led to the scientific revolution.

Chapter 6 deals with the quintessentially defining characteristic of scientific knowledge. The quantification of natural phenomena is introduced and explained using the evolving understanding of motion as an example; this naturally allows the reader to see that it was the efforts to understand motion properties that brought about the scientific revolution. The conviction that nature can ultimately yield its secrets through mathematical representations and the origins of the use of models are dealt with; the limitations inherent in the practice of one of the most salient features of scientific explanations, reductionism, are also highlighted.

A section follows with chapters on the philosophical features that have come to define science as a distinctive way to look at nature, particularly in terms of methodological improvements over the previous views. Chapter 7 is designed to illustrate that, just as the use of logic during the scholastic period began as a means of strengthening sacred scripture but could also be used to undermine it, the use of scientific knowledge to account for human nature can lead to a similar undermining of traditional views of our place in the scheme of things. The objective is to demonstrate to the reader that scientific knowledge can be misused, such as when pronouncements are made based on scientific knowledge that aren't themselves scientific. Examples are given of instances of scientism and how to properly assess claims made in the name of science that may actually be a misappropriation of its epistemic authority.

Chapter 8 provides a continuation of the concluding tone of the previous one with the intent of demonstrating how it is that scientific methodology has turned out to be so crucially important in providing naturalistic accounts of phenomena. There is a brief discussion of the logical basis of scientific explanations, combined with a demonstration of the tentative nature of science—in other words, that scientific knowledge is by definition incomplete and subject to revision. There are significant pedagogical implications that follow this discussion, and suggestions are offered for ways to introduce students to the methodological foundations of scientific knowledge and practice.

Chapter 9 contains the thrust of my approach to dispel a common misconception among students that is largely a pedagogical consequence and that likely inhibits the inherently fascinating nature of scientific practice—namely, that typical science instruction emphasizes factual knowledge and fails to convey to students how little is actually known about the universe. Science is no doubt constituted by a body of knowledge, but it is also a unique way of seeing the world that involves critical thinking. I share the conviction held by many that we could be more successful in promoting scientific literacy and producing more reflective citizens if we effectively convey to students how little we know about what is potentially knowable.

The concluding section contains chapters designed to demonstrate the single most inexorable character of scientific knowledge: its applications. It is in this part that we take a more critical view of the significance of what it means to "know" anything scientifically. The objective is to provide the basis for students to see that, despite all its accomplishments, there are limitations to science as an explanatory structure and, perhaps more importantly, there are many *inappropriate* extensions that constitute the basis for scientism.

In chapter 10, the philosophical implications of twentieth-century physical theories are emphasized with the intent to illustrate the difficulties in understanding microscopic phenomena that successful scientific theories have generated, despite the enormous improvements made over earlier attempts to understand nature, particularly at the macroscopic level. This discussion provides the basis for the consideration of one of the main themes of the book: that there may be limits to what scientific knowledge can provide, largely due to its provisional character.

In chapter 11, the metaphysical aspects of scientific knowledge are emphasized as a result of the philosophical issues discussed in the previous chapter. The goal is to provide the reader with a larger context where science can be more readily seen as a human activity, and that based on sociological and philosophical considerations should be more encompassing of alternative explanatory structures. A particularly desirable outcome would be to allow the reader to see that dogmatism is to be avoided in scientific knowledge if humanity is to continue to benefit from its use to solve our most pressing problems.

Chapter 12 shows that the emergence of the perception of the unquestionable authority of science at its beginnings exhibits a similar pattern to our current expectation that science can provide the answers to all our questions about the universe. However, such an oversimplification of the significance of science in the larger context of human affairs must be resisted if we are to continue to benefit from its achievements, while at the same time allowing for an understanding of its limitations, as modern societies ought to believe.

~

Acknowledgments

A book about a topic deemed incomplete and subject to revision is unlikely to escape its own premise. Consequently, any omissions and areas found to be in need of improvement are solely the author's responsibility. Nevertheless, since my intent has been to provide the reader with some intellectual stimulation, any measure of success in this regard must be attributed to the contributions and valuable feedback provided by many individuals. Among these are students and colleagues who have participated in informal and organized discussions about the topic. In particular I wish to thank Professor Russell Bradshaw of Lehman College for his insights and suggestions and Professor James Llana of John Jay College of Criminal Justice, who while at Old Westbury provided considerable advice on an early draft of the book.

While I dedicate this work to my family, I want to specifically thank Michael Aymar for his impeccable editing help; not only does he have a good grasp of my ideas, but he allowed them to flow freely in many instances. I also wish to thank my son Gerard for his drawing and my maternal grandfather Antonio, who long ago encouraged in me the pursuit of philosophical inquiry.

~

Introduction

The purpose of this book is to provide the reader with opportunities to acquire and reflect on a perspective in which science can be properly understood as a system comprised of a body of knowledge, a way of looking at nature, and a means to describe and hopefully explain it. It has been my experience after many years of teaching that we teachers continually underestimate our students' capacity for being intrigued by what is mysterious about reality. We (mis)manage to do this by conveying to them through our teaching the seemingly unavoidable authoritative nature of science, while concomitantly failing to highlight the inherently tentative and limited scope that it has in explaining the universe.

The last statement may seem surprising given what one may experience through technological applications of scientific discoveries. What could be more obvious than that the amount of information available to the typical person in modern societies is orders of magnitude greater than what most people have known through the ages?

In recent years, the larger issue in education has become *what to do* with the knowledge ostensibly acquired in schools and institutions of higher learning. This is particularly important with scientific knowledge, since individuals are expected to require increasingly demanding critical thinking, or problem-solving skills, in dealing with most aspects of modern life. A good starting point for our discussion can be a distinction between *data, information*, and *knowledge* and, perhaps as the culmination of all these, the use of *wisdom* in making decisions.

Definitions of the above items can be found in any dictionary; however, for the purpose of our discussion, we should concentrate on their most important applications: critical thinking and wisdom. *Critical thinking* can be thought of as a way to form an opinion based on at least two perspectives; *wisdom* can then be seen as the use of three or more perspectives. It is undeniable that, in the modern world, knowledge has become fragmented due to specialization. Consequently, critical thinking can be seen to have an important property: it allows for a transition between knowledge and understanding.[1]

Students have access to much more information outside of school than in their learning settings—a fact that makes the use of critical thinking a necessity. We can agree that understanding is more desirable than information or even knowledge; however, without the ability to think critically, one can't exercise *discernment*—the ability to make judgments and an integral feature of understanding.[2] This is all the more important when assessing information such as is provided by the Internet, perhaps the most popular source of information (as well as misinformation?) available to date.

The basis of critical thinking is reflection, something that I consider to be more important than the acquisition of knowledge itself. Therefore, I have included in each chapter opportunities for reflection, a task in the chapter and another at the end. I believe that the most important skill teachers can help students develop in any discipline is the ability to be reflective. This means that, as you read on, you must be actively engaged with the material, not just a passive participant. I hope that you will be critical of ideas and concepts that you find difficult to believe or accept, but only *after* you have reflected on them. My intent is to allow you to see that science and scientific knowledge can be subjected to criticism and not just simply accepted. This is particularly important when you are confronted with statements made in the name of science, by nonscientists and scientists alike, that are, strictly speaking, *unscientific*.

A lack of critical thinking also leaves one at the mercy of individuals and groups with agendas that do not have one's best interests in mind. Their objectives, often commercial or political, can generally be considered detrimental due to their power to manipulate emotions while inhibiting reflection.

Think of examples of what constitutes *data*, *information*, *knowledge*, and *wisdom*. Is there a progression from data to wisdom? In other words, is there a *flow* one way? Where would you include *understanding* in that sequence?

It is crucial to be able to exercise critical thinking in the manner just described, since there are many ways that scientific knowledge can be misused and can inappropriately convey an air of authority in areas where it is not warranted. There is an urgent need for citizens to engage in critical views of the many applications of scientific knowledge where societal issues are at stake. If one doesn't develop the skills to do this, democratic principles could be compromised and even our very freedoms jeopardized. This may sound extreme, but as you read on, you'll see that having these skills is what is required to be a functional member of society. Leaving all important decisions to "experts" renders the general populace mere participants in life, rather like spectators at a sporting event—except, of course, that the issues at stake are much more serious than any game.

Items for Reflection

- To give an example of activities that can be done with the items in the box on page 2, consider the following questions: (1) Does data processing lead to information? (2) Does the accumulation of factual information lead to knowledge?
- A distinction has been made between uses of the term *wisdom*. A traditional view held that to display wisdom is to make decisions following the rules of logic; a more contemporary view holds that to display wisdom is to make effective decisions while operating in an environment of uncertainty. Do you agree with such a distinction?

CHAPTER ONE

The Need for Scientific Literacy

One of the greatest needs of the world in our time is the growth and widespread dissemination of a true historical perspective, for without it whole peoples can make the gravest misjudgements about each other. Since science and its application dominate so much our present world, since men of every race and culture take so great a pride in man's understanding and control over her, it matters vitally to know how this modern science came into being. Was it purely a product of the genius of Europe, or did all civilizations bring their contributions to the common pool? A right historical perspective here is one of the most urgent necessities of our time.

—Joseph Needham

Scientific literacy has become a professional imperative in the modern world. Most professions have come to depend a great deal on advances in scientific and technological research. Scientifically trained individuals presumably have extensive exposure to those features of knowledge about science and technology that are essential for the possession of scientific literacy. However, the average citizen will most likely feel that such literacy cannot be acquired absent formal scientific training. Nevertheless, the need to understand issues involved in discussions of man's impact on the environment, the definition of a mental illness, the social implications of medical practice, and the use of genetic information about individuals, to name a few instances, requires varying degrees of scientific literacy.

The need for scientific literacy stems from the increasingly obvious impact of science in just about every aspect of human existence in the modern world. As an example, consider the fact that quantum mechanics, one of the most important scientific theories developed in the twentieth century, has been primarily of interest to scholars due to its importance in modern physical science aspects concerning microscopic measurements. However, recent developments in nanotechnology and the miniaturization of many devices require that business and engineering professionals know more about quantum theory and its applications than ever before. Inventions such as the transistor, the laser, magnetic resonance imaging (MRI), and the inevitable quantum computer of the future are just a few of the applications that follow from esoteric quantum theory.[1]

Despite the acknowledged utility of emerging and evolving technological applications of scientific discoveries,[2] many surveys indicate that a vast majority of people have little, if any, understanding of science and how it has come to play such a dominant role in modern existence.[3] Curiously, most people express respect for and confidence in scientific information, from legal and medical testimony in courts of law to a general feeling of acceptance toward any claim declared to have a scientific basis. Yet this attitude is based more on ignorance or sheer intimidation caused by the perceived difficulty and complexity of scientific work that naturally begins to take shape as the population encounters science formally as part of the traditional educational experience.

The issue is not just of academic interest and importance. It has become more pressing in the modern world, as there are calls for a rethinking of the context of the traditional relationship between science and society due to the increasing complexity of the interactions between scientific discoveries, along with their technological applications, and the nonexpert community.[4] In fact, it can be argued that the reliance by society on the opinions of experts can be dangerous to democracies. When the public cannot participate in the debates between contending groups of specialists, the autonomy of ordinary citizens in a democracy is seriously compromised.[5] The dialogue must be mutual—research and innovation must heed what society considers useful—as opposed to the traditional dissemination of scientific knowledge to the public. Of course, this requires a considerable measure of scientific literacy among the populace.

Scientific literacy is necessary for prospective science teachers in particular and for college students in general. The debate between a belief in the creation of life by a divine being and the empirical evidence for the theory of evolution during the past hundred years illustrates not only the extent to which the general public misunderstands the issues involved but also the mutual mistrust exhibited by most proponents of the two views. In its most recent version, the debate has been between the proponents of intelligent design, an intellectually sophisticated movement considered by scientists to be a form of creationism, and evolutionary theory.[6] The arguments offered by intelligent design proponents are not restricted to just those from evolutionary biology; there are mathematicians and philosophers of science involved as well. The most visible confrontations have been in situations concerning the biology curriculum offerings in public school districts.[7]

The aim of this book is to provide students and other readers with a context for an understanding of science, maintaining a balance between a scholarly approach that necessarily requires a detailed study of several disciplines and a presentation geared toward a general audience that, despite the gravity of the topic, needs *for its own self-interest* to understand many of the concepts discussed. The context, as the title indicates, is provided by two essential aspects of scientific knowledge and practice: first, the *nature* of science, which can be understood by demonstrating its philosophical and social origins, as well as the construction and confirmation of theories; and second, its *development*, which can best be demonstrated by a historical analysis of its emergence and evolution as a distinctive way of knowing and dealing with the natural world.

A central theme in the evolution of scientific knowledge is the idea of progress. Students must understand that knowledge systems developed by other cultures and often called "science" lack this idea of progress as a greater dominion over nature. The technological aspects of scientific practice can also be incorporated into this approach, particularly in terms of its application and societal implications. Therefore, these aspects can be discussed after the alternatives have been investigated. Diverse cultures have contributed scientific knowledge and technological inventions throughout history; however, the debate concerning multiculturalism and the apparent universality of scientific knowledge can be best understood *after* students realize that they must first understand *modern Western science* before they can appreciate the value of other cultural views and contributions.

The need for a context necessitates that students engage in a limited but considerable analysis and reflection of philosophical issues and historical events. To this extent, philosophical definitions are unavoidable. A proper understanding of the terminology is essential if one is to grasp how science arose and how it has become the basis for the idea of progress, an idea prevalent in Western nations and perhaps one of the reasons for the conflict between traditional spiritual beliefs and modern life.

The late philosopher of science Sir Karl Popper (1902–1994) considered the growth of human knowledge during the past three hundred years to be largely the result of the growth in scientific knowledge.[8] Such a sweeping statement can be justified when one compares the relative growth in knowledge of any other discipline to that in scientific areas. While some writers may claim that this growth in knowledge has not necessarily translated into more understanding in many areas, it is nevertheless undeniable that the sheer accumulation of knowledge about nature and the universe at large have revolutionized the way humans have come to see the world. Yet surveys of public understanding of issues that involve scientific knowledge and how these relate to human affairs show that most industrialized nations are in a rather peculiar situation: despite centuries of growth in our knowledge about the natural world, a significant portion of the population appears to have more confidence and certainty about their *beliefs* about reality than about their *knowledge* of it.

National organizations have been advocating the development of a scientifically literate population as one of the most pressing needs in industrialized nations. However, what causes anxiety among many when confronted with the realization of the significance of scientific knowledge in most professions is the conclusion that, without a scientific training, this type of literacy may be unattainable. Even those who have been exposed to scientific training through the traditional methods of science instruction are usually told *what* we know and not *how* we have come to know it. The emphasis on conveying factual information at the expense of processes of knowing gives students the impression that scientific knowledge cannot be improved upon, and thus they develop that sense of acceptance in the face of authority, which shortchanges their understanding of science.

An aspect of science that is often absent in academic presentations and in the way the media portray scientific work is the incredibly dramatic way in which it has become such a dominant view of reality in the modern world. The inherently exciting historical aspects of science's emergence as a distinctive way of seeing the world have been neglected. There are countless opportunities to "tell a good story" when considering how discoveries about the natural world have been made, particularly when breakthroughs have come about by chance. By identifying points in time that demonstrate clear connections among various disciplines, students can realize the authentic interdependency of skills and knowledge that constitute scientific inquiry.

The outline of such an approach can be constructed by initially providing a "scaffolding" or structure where the essential concepts, definitions of terms, and general ideas are introduced. This is followed by case studies of certain disciplines where singular events or series of occurrences are presented to show how they led to discoveries or advances in understanding of the discipline, as well as the links to other areas, thus resulting in an interdisciplinary treatment of the development of scientific ideas. Some examples of tasks designed to expose students to historically important experiments and their eventual modern interpretation and approach are included in appendix A.

The thrust of my approach is to make it clear that science is a human activity that is essentially a 350-year-old way of looking at nature, and as such, it is as likely to continue on its path of discovery as it is to turn into a perspective on the universe that we can only imagine at this time and that may look quite different from the way we envision science today. This latter point seems particularly difficult for students to understand, as many of them see scientific knowledge as rigid and absolute—not as incomplete and subject to revision, as it has been traditionally intended by its practitioners.

An awareness of three fundamental characteristics of scientific knowledge can serve as the basis for a development of scientific literacy for all students willing to engage in studying the way science arose and continues to evolve. These are:

1. Scientific explanations must be *naturalistic* (which is based on ancient Greek attempts, on the resurgence of an interest in the study of nature in western Europe during the early twelfth century, and on the fact that science emerged from "natural philosophy").
2. Scientific hypotheses must be *as simple as possible* (which is based on the thirteenth-century principle of "parsimony" or "Ockham's razor").
3. Scientific claims must be *testable* (which is based on Galileo's emphasis in the seventeenth century on experimental work as the decisive test of knowledge claims).[9]

It should be noted that the first two features are not exclusively displayed by scientific practice; other forms of knowledge could include these aspects as well. However, the third one is the definitive feature of science, provided it is applicable. In scientific areas that have a historical character, the testability criterion can't be applied in the same way that it can in empirical areas where experimental conditions can be replicated. This has led to the idea of a hierarchy in the sciences that dates back almost two hundred years.[10] In this view, scientific disciplines differ in complexity and generality, which perhaps gives the nonscientific population the impression that some theories are less likely to be true if they come from those disciplines regarded as belonging to the so-called soft sciences.[11]

Consider a common misconception concerning the nonscientific understanding of the term *theory*. Many people appear to make a distinction between accepting two prominent theories: gravitation and evolution. The fact that gravitation and its effects can be more readily experienced than evolution and its effects leads them to conclude that gravitation is a more firmly established theory. If experiences lead one to accept one theory rather than another, then perhaps it is the experiences that should be questioned, since one should either accept or reject a theory on the basis of the evidence. The intuitive or counterintuitive aspects of some theories contribute more to their acceptance or rejection by the general population than do the detailed analyses that are usually undertaken by scientists.

Nevertheless, testability became decisive in science when the earliest scientific societies proclaimed their rejection of knowledge claims based on authority. An example is provided by the Royal Society of London, established in 1660, whose motto, *"Nullius in Verba,"* asserts the rejection of anyone's verbal authority.[12] This last feature is significant in light of the fact that, as already pointed out, many students and adults appear to regard scientific knowledge as possessing unquestionable authority, thus betraying the intentions of its initial and current practitioners. The empirical testability of even the "hardest" sciences has been questioned,[13] and this should be made explicit to students at various stages of their exposure to scientific knowledge.

The current public debate between advocates for creation and those for evolution appears to reside in a mutual misunderstanding of the authority of scientific claims. Many statements that are made by both scientists and nonscientists about the meaning of existence, the spiritual nature of humanity, the apparent lack of purpose in nature, and so forth, can meet the first two criteria of scientific knowledge but not the third. Thus they go beyond the authority that science legitimately has earned as a type of knowledge. Statements not meeting the third criterion can be made in the name of science, but they cannot be regarded as scientific. If they seem to have an air of authority, it is because of a perception that scientific statements are somehow "closer to the truth" (whatever that means). Statements in this category are an example of *scientism*—the misuse and application of statements from science in areas where they may not legitimately apply. As such, these statements ought to be regarded as having as much authority as their opposites and should be debated accordingly. It is therefore essential that we develop a clear understanding of what exactly it is that makes scientific knowledge unique.

A survey of the development of ideas in various disciplines that is based on a philosophical and historical analysis of certain events can become

The phenomenon of extra-sensory perception or ESP, by which individuals claim to be able to communicate or learn information solely through mental powers, is not currently viewed as meeting the criteria for a scientific explanation. Can you think of reasons why this is the case?

the forum or medium through which students gain the much-needed appreciation and understanding of science and thus are able to obtain a good measure of scientific literacy, along with the acquisition of a proper way to see science as a human activity. The organization of this book is meant to provide teachers with opportunities to engage students in those areas deemed essential by the National Science Teachers Association to convey the nature of science through its history, philosophy, and practice. Teachers must also enable students to distinguish science from other forms of knowledge, to understand the evolution and practice of science as a human endeavor, and to look critically at claims and assertions made in the name of science.

At the same time, one of the goals of the National Science Education Standards can be fulfilled when students understand that, despite all its advances, there are certain things that science *cannot* do. An understanding of science also involves a consideration of whether there is a limit to human knowledge about the natural world, particularly since, at least in their popularized versions, what are considered significant scientific conclusions about the natural world appear to verge on becoming answers to the "big questions." However, there also needs to be a consideration of the possibility that some of these questions may not be answerable. If one thinks that the ultimate answers to questions about the natural world can be provided by science, it would be worthwhile to remember the words of the great biologist Sir Peter Medawar (1915–1987), who admonished us to keep in mind that, while there are very few problems in modern life where scientific evidence is not relevant, there are also very few problems where scientific evidence is *all* the evidence needed.[14]

The objective of this chapter has been to establish that scientific literacy is a modern professional imperative. However, scientific literacy isn't limited to the acquisition of scientific knowledge; it also requires an understanding of the impact that science has come to have on most aspects of life. The particular view of progress that has resulted from a dominion over nature has created a definite need for us to understand what science can legitimately do and what it cannot do.

It is important to demonstrate that science is the result of human activities that can often be traced to ancient practices, contrary to the impression held by many that humanity suddenly experienced an awakening from ignorance during the scientific revolution of the seventeenth century in Europe. To do this, we need to broaden our understanding of the evolution of science and its forerunners. This, in turn, means that we need to consider many ancient historical and prehistoric events, including the earliest documented attempts to use tools, the subsequent impact of early forms of technology on human evolution, and the many discoveries that have inevitably shaped the ways various cultures and civilizations emerged and developed. We can accomplish this with the help of a chronological organization of important events dating back to the earliest known facts about the Earth.

Items for Reflection

- Make a list of ten activities you engage in daily that would be impossible without modern technology.
- Several national organizations consider the lack of scientific literacy among the general population in the United States to be a threat to national security and to the future of the nation. Can you think of three reasons why this perception exists?

For Further Reading

Derry, G. N. *What Science Is and How It Works*. Princeton, NJ: Princeton University Press, 1999.

Horgan, J. *The End of Science: Facing the Limits of Knowledge in the Twilight of the Scientific Age*. Reading, MA: Addison-Wesley, 1996.

Miller, K. *Finding Darwin's God: A Scientist's Search for Common Ground Between God and Evolution*. New York: Cliff Street Books/HarperCollins, 1999.

CHAPTER TWO

~

The Origins of Accomplishing Tasks

From Individual to Organized Efforts

As was stated in the previous chapter, we need a wider perspective on how science emerged from earlier and different views of nature. That means we must consider a number of events that were decisive in humanity's ability to understand and control many natural phenomena and eventually translated into the technologically dominated modern world. This chapter will detail the background necessary to begin an analysis of the *development* of scientific knowledge.

Such background can be provided by a survey of prehistoric events that resulted in technological improvements facilitated by the earliest known use of tools. It is known that other species use tools to accomplish certain tasks, but when compared to humans, the twigs, branches, and stones used by chimpanzees to obtain food seem sporadic behavior. It is unique among early humans to have developed and improved tools for purposes related to *survival*.

An early example of the tools made exclusively by humans is the stone flake, which facilitated changes in diet, habitat, and biological functions. The use of the flakes chipped from stone by the earliest known toolmakers has been shown to make cutting and butchering large prey much easier than was possible with other available materials. Evidence from the chipping of stones and the types of flakes produced that has been discovered at certain archaeological sites has led to a fascinating conclusion about when humans developed "handedness"—87 percent of humans today are right-handed, 13 percent left-handed, compared to the observed 50:50 ratio among chimpanzees—placing this event or series of events at between 1.9 and 1.5 million years ago.[1] The way the chipping was done before 1.9 million years ago shows a roughly equal ratio of striking the rocks with the right and left hands; however, at some point the chipping begins to show a preference for striking the rock with the right hand. The evidence can be interpreted as a shift in handedness, with most flakes being the product of right-handed efforts. The profound implications of this shift for the eventual different functions of the human brain's hemispheres are obvious and can serve to illustrate the dramatically different ways from other primates in which humans have proceeded in the documented evolution of the species; right-handed far outnumber left-handed individuals in human societies.

Of course, the use of stone tools evolved. The most primitive examples include tools to work wood that are believed to have been used in Equatorial Africa between 200,000 and 100,000 years ago. The evolution continued to hafted hand axes and cleavers (stone tools inserted or attached to a handle) before culminating with ground stone axes around 20,000 years before metals appear to have been used.[2]

There are many other significant prehistoric inventions that have been documented; among these are the use of fire, the bow and arrow, the wheel, and a number of hand tools, including the boomerang in Australia, the toggle-joint harpoon of the Eskimos, and the manioc squeezer in South America. Numerous examples of contemplative and creative ways to understand nature have been found in caves where humans spent a great portion of their time; however, it is during the Neolithic era (around 8000 BCE) in the Middle East, with the development of agriculture and writing that a decisive difference between hunter-gatherers (nomads), and protofarmers (sedentary) appears. It is then that human beings seem to have begun to undertake most of the activities that led to the earliest attempts to manipulate their surroundings and the environment. With the development of agriculture, population increases gave rise to the earliest civilizations around river basins. Irrigation became a most important activity. Roads and communication links became necessary so that centralized power could be effectively exercised.

Table 2.1 is a chronology of some of the most significant events spanning time measured in terms of the known periods of archaeology and the epochs and eras of geology. The dates included are an approximation, since there is disagreement among scientists as to the exact dates on the geologic time scale.

An analysis of table 2.1 can illustrate several interesting features of our knowledge about events in the history of the Earth that are relevant to an understanding of the nature of scientific answers in the larger context of human knowledge, such as the origins of life and the development of humans.

Table 2.1. Chronological Display of Significant Events in Earth's Distant Past

Millions of years ago	Event	Period/Era/Epoch	
4,500	Formation of Earth's lithosphere (oldest known rocks)	Pre-Cambrian ("earliest era") Azoic (4,568–3800) period	
4,000	Formation of primordial sea; first single-celled life forms (algae and bacteria) appear in water	Archeozoic and Protozoic (3,800–570) periods/eras	
800	First oxygen-breathing animals appear; development of interdependent specialized cells		
600	Invertebrate multicelled animals having shells; first plants on land	Paleozoic ("ancient life") Cambrian (570–505), Ordovician (505–438), and Silurian (438–408) periods	
400	Amphibians move onto land; earliest reptiles and insects	Devonian (408–360), Carboniferous [Mississippian and Pennsylvanian] (360–286), and Permian (286–245) periods	
200	Early dinosaurs		
200–100	Dinosaurs, birds, and mammals	Mesozoic ("middle life") Triassic (245–208), Jurassic (208–144), and Cretaceous (144–65) periods	
65	Prosimians, early primates in trees	Cenozoic ("recent life") Epochs Paleocene (65–58) and Eocene (58–37)	
40	Monkeys and apes evolve; *Catopithecus browni* (~40), *Aegyopithecus* (~30), *Proconsul* (~20)	Oligocene (37–24) and Miocene (24–5)	
10	*Ramapithecus* in Africa and India	Pliocene (5–2)	
6	*Australopithecus* (*africanus, afarensis, robustus*) in Africa		
	[*Because of a gap in the human fossil records, beginning around 10 million years ago, the ancestry of all hominids is relatively difficult to trace*]	**Geological period**	**Archaeological period**
2 1.5 1.0	*Homo habilis* Oldest known tools fashioned in Africa *Homo erectus* emerges in Africa and East Indies *Homo erectus* populates temperate zones	Lower Pleistocene	Lower Paleolithic (*oldest period of the old stone age*)

(continued)

Table 2.1. *(Continued)*

Thousands of years BCE			
800	Humans learn to control and use fire Large-scale elephant hunts Humans begin to make artificial shelters	Middle Pleistocene	Lower Paleolithic
400	Neanderthals emerge in Europe		
100			
	Ritual burials in Europe and Near East suggest belief in afterlife; woolly mammoths hunted	Upper Pleistocene	Middle Paleolithic (*middle period of the old stone age*)
60	In Europe, cave bear becomes focus of cult; Cro-Magnon arises		
40		L A S T	
		I C E	
		A G E	Upper Paleolithic (*latest period of old stone age*)
35	Asian hunters cross Bering land bridge to New World; oldest known written record in central Africa (lunar notations on bone); humans reach Australia; art in caves in France and Spain		
30	Figurines for nature worship; counting begins in Europe		
20	Invention of needle; bison hunting in North America; sheep/goats domesticated in the Near East		
10	Bow and arrow invented; pottery first made in Japan; Near East: pigs and cattle domesticated, a system of counting using baked clay tokens begins.	Holocene	Mesolithic (*middle stone age*)

Years BCE			
9,000			
	Dog domesticated in Mesopotamia		
8,000			
	Jericho, oldest known city, settled; goat domesticated in Persia; cultivation of first crops, wheat and barley, in Near East	Holocene	Neolithic (*new stone age*)
7,000	Pattern of village life grows in the Near East		
6,000	Cattle domesticated in Near East; agriculture begins to replace hunting in Europe		
5,000	Horse domesticated in Ukraine Copper used in trade in Mediterranean areas; corn cultivated in Mexico		
4,800	Oldest known massive stone monument built in Brittany	Holocene	Copper Age
4,000	Sail-propelled boats used in Egypt; first city-states develop in Sumer		
3,500	First potatoes grown in South America; wheel and plow originate in Sumeria; rice begins to be cultivated in Far East		
3,000	Bronze first used to make tools in Near East; city life spreads in Near East; Egyptian calendar		
2,800	Stonehenge; pyramids in Egypt; Minoan navigators venture into areas beyond Mediterranean		Bronze Age
2,600	Variety of gods and heroes; Gilgamesh, other epics in Near East; silkworm cultivation begins in China	Holocene	
2,500	Cities rise in Indus Valley; earliest written code of laws (Hammurabi) in Sumer; herdsmen in Central Asia learn to tame and ride horses		

(continued)

Table 2.1. *(Continued)*

2,000	Use of bronze in Europe; chicken and elephant domesticated in Indus Valley; Eskimo culture develops in the Bering Strait area		Bronze Age
1,500	Invention of oceangoing canoes; islands of South Pacific reached; ceremonial bronze sculptures in China; imperial government established by Hittites		
1,400	Iron in use in Near East; first complete alphabet devised in script of the Ugarit in Syria; introduction of concept of monotheism by Hebrews	Holocene	Iron Age
1,000	Reindeer domesticated in Eurasia		
900	Modern alphabet developed by Phoenicians; natural gas from wells used in China; first symbol for zero (as a place holder) used in India		
800	Celtic culture begins to spread; use of iron throughout Europe; creation of a far-flung society by nomads based on the horse in Russian steppes; first highway system built in Assyria; Homer composes the *Iliad* and the *Odyssey*		
700	Foundation of Rome; wheelbarrow invented in China		
200	*Mahabharata, Ramayana*; waterwheel invented in Near East		
0	Common Era begins		

Sources: J. L. Kulp, "Geologic Time Scale," *Science* 133, no. 3459 (1961): 1105–14; R. H. Dott and R. L. Batten, *Evolution of the Earth*, 4th ed. (New York: McGraw-Hill, 1988); P. Barnes-Svarney, *The New York Public Library Science Desk Reference* (New York: Macmillan, 1995).

The earliest part of the table indicates that we seem to have a pretty good idea of *when* life began, judging from what is known about the early Earth; however, we don't know *how* life began. There is some empirical evidence for an origin of life based on experimental results from laboratory simulations of the early Earth environment, in which simple chemical substances with the help of electricity spontaneously produced organic materials found in living systems. Nevertheless, it is unlikely that these experiments demonstrate that life began exactly this way. Besides the view of the origin of life based on the idea of divine creation, there are other speculative theories that the origin of life might even be extraterrestrial.

The issue of human origins, although less uncertain, shares a similar level of controversy. There is abundant empirical evidence for the emergence and evolution of the human species, despite known gaps in the fossil record, as indicated in the table. This is an area where there is a lack of understanding of the evidence among many proponents of the creation view. The main issue of contention is not about the origins and evolution of the human species, since many religious thinkers accept the theory of evolution commonly referred to as the Darwinian Theory. The real issue is about the origin of *life itself*, since most of the scientific uncertainty in knowledge resides here.

Recent debates have postulated views that current scientific knowledge may be reaching a "plateau"—a period when discoveries as important as those made in the twentieth century seem increasingly unlikely. This highlights the feeling among some critics that science itself may be incapable of answering such fundamental questions as the origin of life.

The issues just listed, based on the table, serve to illustrate the need for a proper understanding of the emergence of science as the most distinctively "progressive" way humans have found to cope with the many material challenges they have faced. A look at the earliest attempts to understand the natural world can help us to see how this type of knowledge evolved to become the most productive means to deal with the physical world. Our analysis of the impact of ancient knowledge on the eventual emergence of modern science would necessarily require that we spend some time studying those early civilizations in recorded history—namely, the Chinese, Indian,

---

The theory that life has an extraterrestrial origin has both supporters and critics. Despite many claims in the media about visits from aliens, there is no conclusive scientific evidence that life on Earth has come from outer space. However, if such evidence were provided, what problem would still remain?

Mesopotamian, and Egyptian—where abundant scholarship on their general knowledge base has been done.

The civilizations around the Euphrates River are older than those around the Nile. However, compared to the Egyptian civilization, not much information about many of their particular activities is preserved, although there are many tablets that give information about certain aspects of life. One probable reason is that the Egyptians had abundant limestone and granite, while Mesopotamia lacks stone and does not have much good timber. Therefore, most structures were made of sun-dried mud bricks. The fascination with the cycles of the moon gave rise to the earliest calendars, and concepts related to numbers and counting appeared soon after agriculture was invented. In fact, some scholars claim that writing may have developed out of the necessity to keep accurate records of commercial transactions.

The first engineering works in Mesopotamia were the irrigation canals. The first recorded engineering work in Egypt is the wall of the city of Memphis, at the point of the Nile Delta. Before discussing other monumental works, however, we must note megalithic (meaning "made of large stones") structures developed for astronomical purposes. The largest of such structures, Carnac, is located in Brittany in northern France; a stone weighing more than 300 tons and being about 70 feet long, broken into five pieces (one of which is missing) appears to be a sighting guide for lunar position observations, particularly "standstills" (maximum positions of the moon in the sky measured from the celestial equator). The most famous megalithic structure is, of course, Stonehenge in England. It seems that approximately a thousand years elapsed between its initial phase and its completion, resulting in phases that archaeoastronomers have called Stonehenge I (beginning around 2800 BCE), Stonehenge II (beginning around 2100 BCE), and Stonehenge III (beginning around 2000 BCE). Both amateur and professional speculations have concluded, based on alignments, that its purpose was mainly to keep track of the motions of the sun and the moon, thus allowing for accurate preparation for planting and harvesting, as well as predicting eclipses.

Before the rise of cities, dwellings were built in the Middle East by placing circular arrangements of studs or vertical rods and filling the spaces between these supports with clay to form a wall, as shown in figure 2.1.

With the development of cities, these dwellings became rectangular in shape, with bricks now serving as the material used to make the walls. The world's first mass-production device appears to have been the Sumerian (early Mesopotamian) brick.[3]

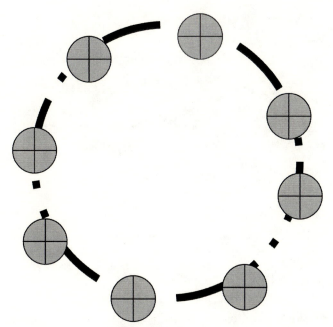

Figure 2.1. A circular arrangement of vertical posts with the space between them filled in with clay provided the earliest type of dwelling in the Middle East.

A legitimate question at this point would be to ask why rectangular dwellings were built and not the familiar circular ones. A look at figure 2.2 shows that this design maximizes the number of dwellings in the given space, since the circular structures have inefficient spaces between them. In other words, there can be more dwellings in the city if they are rectangular than if they are circular. This appears to be an early example of urban planning with the intent to house the largest population in a given area.

Typical choices for dwelling construction were low-elevation sites near water or high-elevation sites atop hills for defensive purposes. Since many sites were in valleys where flooding was a continuous problem, these building practices suggest clear evidence why flood legends are common in early civilizations—examples include the legends of Ziusudra in Sumerian, Utnap-ishtim in Assyrian, Noah in Hebrew, and Deukalion in Greek. In connection with building sites, one of the basic simple machines, the pulley, appears in Mesopotamia before 1500 BCE. It made drawing water from a well much simpler. The most important types of buildings in Mesopotamia were the ziggurats, the most famous of which was Etemanky. Believed to have been

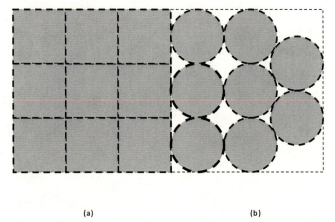

(a)   (b)

Figure 2.2. The two equal areas enclosing (a) squares and (b) circles are seen to differ in the number of dwellings that can be included. The smaller squares and circles have the same length in side and diameter, respectively.

about thirty stories high, it is presumed to be the legendary Tower of Babel. Etemanky was built in honor of Marduk, the chief Babylonian god. Ziggurats evolved from temples, while pyramids in Egypt evolved from tombs.[4]

The extant knowledge of Babylonian science is based predominantly on discoveries of 22,000 clay tablets that come from the ruler Assurbanipal's library (dated to around 626 BCE) and 50,000 tablets from the library of Nippur. Among the most significant contributions of Babylonian civilization is their numerical system, which had a decimal (base-10) system of notation between 1 and 59; the zero does not appear in Mesopotamia until the Persian period (528–330 BCE). For numbers greater than 59, a sexagesimal system (base-60) was used. The sexagesimal system is the device used to this day for angular measurements in astronomy and for fractions of time measurement. The Babylonians also are believed to have invented the concept of the ecliptic (the path followed by the sun in the sky), the sundial, and the water clock and to have made the first record of the constellations. The circle was divided based on the division of the day; the ecliptic was also divided into twelve arcs, giving rise to the zodiac.

In mathematical knowledge, it appears that the quadratic equation

$$(a + b)^2 = a^2 + b^2 + 2ab$$

led the Babylonians to the development of algebra. The advantage of Babylonian mathematics over other systems is the use of the value of place of a number, such as expressed in the following sequence: 1 = 10; 2 = 20; 3 = 30; 4 = 40; 5 = 50; 6 = 1; 7 = 1,10; 8 = 1,20; 9 = 1,30; 10 = 1,40; 11 = 1,50; 12 = 2; 13 = 2,10; and so on. In astronomy, the Babylonians appear to have been primarily interested in the appearance and disappearance of the moon and planets.[5]

The beginning of scientific disciplines, except perhaps astronomy, is closely associated with the invention of writing in Mesopotamia. Chemistry may likely have begun with a documented text from the second millennium BCE that appears to give a recipe for the glazing of pottery.

The most significant contributions of Egyptian civilization to the early forms of scientific knowledge are associated with pyramid building, which lasted until about 1600 BCE. The earliest pyramids appear to have been step structures with the spaces filled in. The building of the pyramids was made possible by expanding knowledge in quarrying, surveying, shaping, and transporting heavy stones, which became a part of the world's first "data base" of technological know-how. Since the Nile River requires considerable management, the Egyptians became accomplished dam and canal builders. In addition to architectural projects, the Egyptians appear to have discovered certain properties of metals around 4000 BCE, as shown by bronze instruments containing approximately 12 percent tin, which is the maximum achievable hardness without fragility. They also discovered the siphon, although there is no evidence that they understood the role of a vacuum.[6]

The introduction of the first practical calendar in Egypt notwithstanding, Egyptian astronomy is believed to have been based on Babylonian observations. The greatest scientific achievements in ancient Egypt are acknowledged to be in mathematics and medicine. The main source of information about Egyptian mathematical contributions is the Rhind papyrus roll, dated to around 1650 BCE although believed to have been copied from an earlier one from 1800 BCE. It contains evidence of a decimal system of notation and of the apparent construction of right triangles from a mathematical relationship that resembles the later Pythagorean Theorem. In medicine, the main sources of information are two papyri. The Edwin Smith papyrus, intended for use by surgeons and dated to possibly around 4000 BCE, contains fragments of a surgical treatise dealing with injuries to the body, beginning with the head and moving down.[7] The Ebers papyrus, from around 1700 BCE, contains recipes for cures intended for use by physicians, consisting of beverages using fruits, vegetables, and animal fats, along with magical songs and rituals.

Ancient medical texts from Babylonian and Egyptian sources make frequent allusions to deities and animals such as falcons and scorpions and

employ the most widely available materials like water and mud as medi-
cines. The Egyptian ones offer much more detail in terms of examination,
diagnosis, and treatment. Some wounds require two or three rounds of the
prescribed medication, citing specific uses of grease, honey, and even the
egg of an ostrich as part of the treatments. There appears to be a striking
contrast between Mesopotamian and Egyptian medicine in that the former
contains many elements of superstition and magic, whereas the latter is more
grounded on naturalistic approaches.[8]

Another highlight of pre-Greek knowledge about the natural world is
Chinese medicine, which interestingly is one of the few non-Western approaches to an understanding of disease and treatment that actually receives
a good deal of attention in modern Western medical institutions and practice. Chinese civilization represents a rather unique perspective by a society
about the need to continue investigating nature after a sophisticated stage
has been achieved. This is a most peculiar situation in the sense that Chinese
thinkers deliberately decided against the continuation of study about nature.[9]
Scholars have determined that Chinese civilization advanced the most technologically between 600 and 1500 CE. Among the known Chinese inventions are papermaking, printing, gunpowder, the mariner's compass, modern
agriculture, shipping, astronomical observatories, decimal mathematics, paper money, umbrellas, wheelbarrows, multistage rockets, brandy and whiskey
(although distillation appears to have been discovered in India), and chess.

Despite the unavoidable omissions due to space and time constraints, we can
demonstrate an instance of the many approaches that different cultures have
employed in their attempts to understand properties of the natural world.
The example is one from mathematics, where documented Chinese and Indian ideas are contrasted to the Mesopotamian development of algebra and,
in a particular case, to the famous Pythagorean Theorem, an idea commonly
associated with Greek mathematical genius.

Pythagoras formulated his famous principle applied to right triangles,
where the sum of the squares of the base A and the height B is equal to the
square of the hypotenuse C:

$$A^2 + B^2 = C^2$$

The same relationship can be obtained in many other ways than the traditional presentation given in mathematics texts that make use of a right
triangle. Two approaches documented to have been undertaken by Chinese
and Indian mathematicians consist of:

1. using squares obtained from rotations of right triangles, and
2. inserting a square within a larger one.

The first approach can be demonstrated by forming a square from the initial right triangle and three other similar triangles arranged adjacent to it. The area of each triangle in figure 2.3 is half the base times the height:

$$\text{Area} = (AB)/2$$

The second similar triangle is rotated by 90° and its base placed so that the height of the first is exactly half the base of the second. Then the third triangle is rotated 180° and placed similarly. Lastly, the fourth is rotated 270° and also placed the same way as the previous ones.

The side of the square inside the four triangles in figure 2.4 is $A - B$, and the area of the square is $(A - B)^2$. The side of the larger square formed by the four triangles is C, and the area of this square is C^2. This is equivalent to adding the area of the inside square and the areas of the four triangles, namely,

$$(A - B)^2 + 4(AB/2) = C^2.$$

Solving this equation, we get

$$A^2 - 2AB + B^2 + 2AB = C^2,$$

from which we get

$$A^2 + B^2 = C^2.$$

The method of inscribing a smaller square into a larger one is illustrated in figure 2.5.

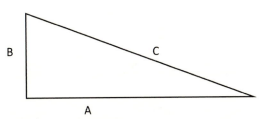

Figure 2.3. Right triangle with base A, height B, and hypotenuse C

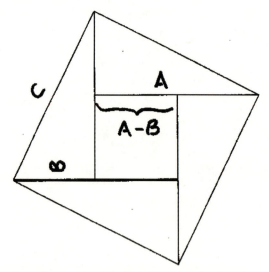

Figure 2.4.   Four right triangles rotated and enclosing a square

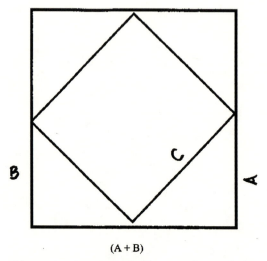

(A + B)

Figure 2.5.   A square of sides A and B enclosing another square of side C

The area of the larger square is $(A + B)^2$, which is equal to the area of the four triangles plus the area of the square inside the larger one. Hence,

$$(A + B)^2 = 4 (AB/2) + C^2.$$

Solving this equation gives

$$A^2 + 2AB + B^2 = 2AB + C^2,$$

which again simplifies to

$$A^2 + B^2 = C^2.$$

Scholars have documented that there are many possible ways that information such as the technique discussed above, could have been disseminated (perhaps via trade routes?) and made its way from one region to another with some alterations. The schematic in figure 2.6 demonstrates how the transmission of information appears to have occurred in different parts of the ancient world, and how the exchange takes place in the modern world.

The model is only a partial representation of the flow of information, since there are other sources (both documented and perhaps yet to be unearthed) of both ancient and more recent knowledge that may have found their way into some of the places and sources that appear in the diagram. A particular case in point is the exchange between European and American (North, Central, and South) ideas, such as the influence of Benjamin Franklin's discoveries in electricity, and the technological innovations brought about by Thomas Edison's laboratory.

In this chapter, I have attempted to demonstrate, through a chronological summary that includes selected prehistoric and ancient events, a larger perspective that shows how scientific knowledge has evolved from views that preceded the seventeenth century. Books on scientific knowledge usually begin with that century as the "officially" accepted beginning of science. This approach, however, fails to acknowledge the many questions about nature that had been entertained before modern science emerged and that continue to be debated. A historical perspective that begins with the seventeenth century is indeed narrow-minded, and the flow chart of knowledge illustrates a much larger perspective by showing how different cultures have influenced *and continue to influence* one another.

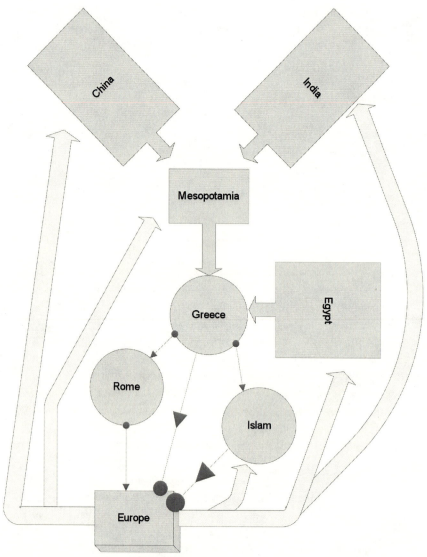

Figure 2.6.   Schematic for the proposed flow of information in the ancient world, and
the modern scientific flow (the broad arrows)

The significance of an analysis of the exchange of information across the planet and its impact on the development of science in western Europe will become evident when we return to it in chapter 5. For now, let us take a good look at the main source of ideas for the development of science from ancient theoretical and experimental knowledge—that of the Greek civilization.

⁓

Items for Reflection

- Why do you think there has been such interest and speculation on how the Egyptian pyramids were built?
- Pyramids had been thought to be exclusively built in Egypt until this practice was also discovered in Central America. Can you think of reasons why this practice was shared by civilizations separated by thousands of miles?

For Further Reading

Barnes-Svarney, P. *The New York Public Library Science Desk Reference.* New York: Macmillan, 1995.

Bernal, J. D. *Science in History.* London: C. A. Watts, 1954.

Gould, R. A., ed. *Explorations in Ethnoarchaeology.* Albuquerque: University of New Mexico Press, 1978.

Joseph, G. G. *Crest of the Peacock: Non-European Roots of Mathematics.* London: I. B. Taurus, 1991.

Neugebauer, O., and A. Sachs. *Mathematical Cuneiform Texts.* New Haven, CT: American Oriental Society and the American Schools of Oriental Research, 1945.

Pfeiffer, J. E. *The Emergence of Society.* New York: McGraw-Hill, 1977.

Toth, N., D. Clark, and G. Ligabue. "The Last Stone Ax Makers." *Scientific American* 267, no. 7 (1992): 88–93.

Unschuld, P. U. *Medicine in China: A History of Pharmaceutics.* Berkeley: University of California Press, 1986.

CHAPTER THREE

~

The Earliest Comprehensive
and Rationalistic Syntheses

The flow of information in the ancient world described in the chart of the previous chapter acquires a particular significance in the case of Greece. Geography has much to do with its strategically central role in the history of ideas, a history that turned out to be critical in the development of science. As can be seen from the schematic and as mentioned in the chapter, there were many contributions made by other civilizations, and these were adapted by the Greeks as a result of the cultural exchanges between these civilizations. Of course, more than the luck of geography is involved in the consideration of the central role of Greek culture in the subsequent exchange of ideas between other very different civilizations.

One aspect of modern life is the complexity of most activities where one is required to think critically, especially when several factors are to be considered for making a proper decision. It has been repeatedly stated that most people are able to *think*, but few are able to *reason*, due to a lack of the ability to *think critically*.[1] This is certainly a problem in a society where many issues of importance depend on an understanding of certain ideas, concepts, principles, and relationships that is impossible to have if one habitually jumps to the quickest and easiest conclusions.

A well-informed society implies more than just one with an abundance of information. Modern nations are certainly in possession of tremendous amounts of information. The problem is what the population needs to do with it to make informed decisions. Among these issues are the environmental impact of human activities on the planet, the use of nonrenewable resources, the consumption of genetically engineered food products, the ethical aspects of certain medical procedures, and the cultural and economic impact of decisions made by governments about issues where data are seriously misrepresented, ideologically manipulated, or both.

An essential component of the technological fruits that have prolonged the human life span and that have enabled and continue to enable humanity to control and exploit many aspects of nature both to improve its lot and to understand its place in the universe is clearly the use of reason. The spiritual dimension of life has traditionally required a reliance on faith as the ultimate resource to discover the truth about reality. The Greeks represent the best example of a civilization that subordinated the reliance on faith to the exercise of reason to try to understand the natural world. An understanding of the nature and development of science requires that one spend a considerable amount of time studying and reflecting on the accomplishments of Greek civilization. It is undeniable that the Greeks are the originators of most intellectual concepts and ideas that the Western world has inherited from antiquity. The scholarship on Greek civilization is vast, and we need to concentrate on the contributions they made to the uses of reason in attempting to understand the world around them. While they borrowed a good deal from other civilizations and groups of people, their uniqueness lies in their discovery of a *methodology* based on a critical study of the rules of reasoning.

The ability to reason requires that we identify our objective, or what the reasoning is going to be about. However, there is a tendency to overestimate the objectivity of one's thought, referred to as the *confirmation bias*—an apparently universal trait of human reasoning that undermines its effectiveness in discovering what may be considered the true nature of reality.[2] Despite the existence of this bias, a goal of Western thought following the tremendous success of the scientific revolution that began in the seventeenth century has been to systematize the various ways we can claim to know anything.

Systematizing knowledge entails an uneasy relationship between the confirmation bias (which involves adherence to what's expected) and skepticism toward traditional knowledge—a willingness to seriously consider new concepts and relationships. These traits constitute an integral part of the creative process. Nonetheless, the increasingly felt desire to systematize knowledge that led to the period known as the Enlightenment can be attributed mainly to the contributions of two seminal thinkers: John Locke (1632–1704) and Immanuel Kant (1724–1804). Their approach compels us to consider what knowledge is and to determine whether we can ever attain it.

We can consider a useful classification of various forms of knowledge that combines modern and traditional views on its acquisition and is based on the assumption that there are four main types, or sources:[3]

1. *Knowledge claims based on authority:* The convictions that result from accepting what traditions and customs have determined to be the truth about reality, as well as the acceptance of the testimony of others sometimes without exercising independent judgment, or without being able to confirm such claims. Most religious views and knowledge about remote world events as well as distant historical events are of this sort.

2. *Knowledge claims based on reasoning:* The convictions arrived at through the exercise of reason using logic. Such claims are believed to enable human beings to discover the fundamental structure of reality after prolonged exercise of individual and collective reasoning. This category is the most significant legacy that Greek civilization has bestowed upon the Western view of the universe. Among the best examples are mathematical knowledge and theoretical quantitative reasoning applied to fundamental questions about existence and about the nature of the universe. A particularly important aspect of reasoning is that it is deductive and thus traditionally seen as superior in providing reliable knowledge. If one begins with *premises*—statements that are demonstrably true—and follows certain rules of thought, it is inevitable that one will get to valid conclusions, that is, statements about reality that are reliably true and that one may not have initially known. This sort of knowledge also constitutes the basis for *rationalism*, the most influential aspect of traditional deliberations about human behavior, ethics, and law.

3. *Knowledge claims based on sense perception:* Convictions arrived at through concrete experiences provided by perception, observation, and reflection upon the information obtained from nature directly or indirectly through the senses. It is based on the principle that *induction*—the conclusion that careful analyses of sensory experiences followed by reasoning—can lead to reliable knowledge. It is also the basis for *empiricism* and *positivism*, views that have shaped modern thinking about nature and human affairs in the West. This sort of knowledge is presumed to be objective and highly responsible for the success of science in providing answers to many questions, although it has led to some counterintuitive views, such as the belief that nothing can exist unless it is somehow observable.

4. *Knowledge claims based on intuition:* Convictions arrived at based on an awareness of acts of consciousness. This type of knowledge serves as a link between types 2 and 3 above, in the sense that having sensory experiences, reflecting on them, and arriving at conclusions that can be trusted requires that a person have a certain confidence that it is he or she who is doing all of the above. Mystical and some religious experiences can result from such awareness following contemplation. A sense of personal identity appears necessary to all forms of knowledge, although intuition alone may not be sufficient to avoid falling into errors about one's conclusions.

We can see that scientific knowledge mainly involves the last three types, but invariably ends up being regarded by many people as containing elements of the first. A clear difference between Western and Eastern views of the universe can be seen in the predominant practice of some of these claims and the emphasis placed on the various types of knowledge. For example, scientific knowledge is mostly based on empirical information (type 3) and logical analysis of it (type 2), whereas Eastern philosophies emphasize intuition (type 4) and tend to regard type 3 as illusory and type 2 often as an obstacle to ultimate knowledge. Of course, many Eastern views rely heavily on authority (type 1), as they have become tradition-bound, although in the case of Buddhism there was a rejection of ancient authority explicitly advocated by the Buddha in his teachings.

It should be emphasized that the most reliable approach to obtaining knowledge that can be considered trustworthy is a combination of all four types of claims, although it is unfortunately often not possible to have evidence from all these either simultaneously or at all.

In order to properly understand the enormous impact of Greek thought on the development of science and the Western view of the universe, we need to state a few definitions about the Greeks' invention of the uses of reason, since these will allow us to see how they went about investigating nature. The most general intellectual activity in the use of reason is the practice of

---

The prophecies of Nostradamus have been extensively discussed in some circles. He is said to have foretold the occurrence of many events that subsequently took place. Regardless of whether the prophecies were indeed true or just coincidences, do you suppose that he could have come to obtain knowledge from a different source than the four discussed above?

philosophy, properly defined as "the love of wisdom." Among its branches, we encounter *epistemology*, the theory of knowledge, concerned with how we come to know anything, and *metaphysics*, an activity of thought that goes beyond what we perceive as reality. Metaphysics concerns the study of things that transcend nature (e.g., abstraction, memory, sensation) and contains the following subdivisions:

- *ontology*, the nature of being, based on the principle of sufficient reason—why any being exists rather than not
- *cosmology*, the inquiry concerned with the study of the origin, large-scale properties, and history of the universe
- *psychology*, the introspective approach to reality based on subjective experiences

The epistemological tradition that originated with the Greeks in their attempts to find the true nature of the universe, including human nature, involves two approaches or views: the *correspondence* and the *coherence* theories of truth. The correspondence theory states that whatever entities we conceive of must match reality; otherwise, our ideas and concepts will end up being simply the fruits of our imagination, without any basis in what is real. This position involves an objective approach based on an ontological assumption of the existence of an independent reality apart from our sensory perceptions and cognitive constructs. The coherence theory requires that we basically must avoid contradicting ourselves in our conclusions about reality, which implies that we don't necessarily have to concern ourselves with whether these have any bearing on what is independently real, thus having an essentially subjective approach.

Since both theories of truth figure prominently in Greek philosophy from its earliest practitioners to the comprehensive systems that incorporated earlier attempts, it is important to understand how they evolved. Consequently, it is convenient to divide the study of Greek ideas into four main chronological stages or periods:[4]

1. The Pre-Socratic Period (700–400 BCE)
2. The period of Plato and Aristotle (fourth century BCE, encompassing Plato's Academy around 388 BCE and Aristotle's Lyceum around 335 BCE)
3. The Hellenistic Period (300–100 BCE)
4. The Greco-Roman Period (100 BCE–400 CE)

For the purpose of understanding the natural world, the Greeks can be said to have had three main approaches:

1. A physical or material approach that emphasized the reality and permanence of matter and movement and allowed for the existence of a vacuum or empty space (Thales, Anaximander, Anaximenes, Democritus).
2. A psychical or formal approach that relied heavily on mathematical reasoning and emphasized the reality and permanence of forms, ideas, and concepts; the senses and perception were considered to have a transitory nature (Pythagoras, Plato).
3. A compromise view where the emphasis was on "becoming," on the actualization of things that exist in potentiality (Aristotle).

The Pre-Socratic Period (700–400 BCE)

The views about the natural world that formed the basis for all subsequent Greek ideas were formulated by the pre-Socratic thinkers or philosophers, who were concerned with the following four major themes:

- What is the nature of the natural world (the entire cosmos) and how did it come into being?
- What is the nature of change? Is reality permanent and change only an illusion?
- What is the nature of perception? Can we trust the senses?
- What is the structure underlying the appearance of the natural world?
- What is it made of? Can it be known?

A list of the pre-Socratic philosophers who were most important for our purposes follows, with a very brief description of their main contributions.[5]

Thales of Miletus (624–547 BCE) represents the earliest known example of a philosopher seeking to develop a comprehensive view of the natural world, arguing that water is the most basic substance or element. He is believed to have predicted an eclipse, probably based on Babylonian information.

Anaximander (611–546 BCE), a disciple of Thales, claimed that the first principle is the infinite. He is the first intellectual to mention that the Earth is suspended freely in space. He is also believed to have drawn the first complete map of the known Earth. Anaximander also discovered the *gnomon*, a device consisting of a stake placed vertically in the ground so that its shadow gives information about the time of day (the principle of the sundial). It is significant that the gnomon provided the opportunity several centuries later to measure the size of the Earth and to determine its circumference with astounding accuracy.

Anaximenes (585/4–528/4 BCE) held that air is the primary element and that stars are fastened to a crystal sphere. He was the first one to mention that the stars carry objects similar to the Earth.

Pythagoras (b. 572 BCE) was the first to hold that the Earth is a sphere and that the planets have a motion independent of the perceived daily rotation, He declared that the morning stars Venus and Mercury were also the evening stars, an idea probably borrowed from Babylonian or Egyptian sources. He held that the universe is spherical and that the Earth is at its center, although his followers later abandoned this view in favor of a model where the Earth and all other celestial objects rotated about an invisible point in space. Pythagoras represents the earliest known example of someone who regards mathematical and deductive reasoning as the ultimate means to understanding the structure of the universe. This seems a natural consequence of his discovery of the principles of harmony in music as being essentially mathematical sequences.

At this point, it is essential to examine in detail two very important sets of opposing views that somehow combine elements from all four questions being debated by the pre-Socratic philosophers. They are the views of Parmenides versus Heraclitus, and those of Empedocles versus Anaxagoras. I must emphasize the enormous significance of these views, since they appear to set the stage for the more sophisticated philosophical systems that follow—those of Plato and Aristotle—and perhaps all successive views. In addition, elements of these views continue to animate and inspire theories and speculation about the nature of the universe, particularly expressed in theoretical physics and modern cosmology.

The most significant contribution of Parmenides (fl. 475 BCE) is his claim that reality must be permanent. A way to state his position is to argue that *whatever changes must not be real*, since by changing, it is at some point in time what it *wasn't* at some other point. In Parmenides' view, reality implies permanence, and therefore anything that changes will come into and go out of existence, thus not being real. This view can be said to be one of an unchanging *substance*, or constancy, and it can be seen to have played a large role in the modern concept of conservation and the physical laws associated with this concept, such as conservation of energy and momentum. It can also be seen as a precursor of the "steady-state" cosmological view of the universe held for a time in twentieth-century astrophysics (now generally discredited in favor of the "Big Bang" theory). The steady-state theory posited that the observable universe has always looked as it currently does and will remain so.

Heraclitus (b. 544 BCE) argued that *change is what is real*. A popular way to state his position is based on his alleged claim: "You cannot step into the same river twice." Properly understood, this implies that, since the water is moving in a river, as opposed to a stagnant body of water, you cannot control its flow. As such, one clearly cannot expect to find the same water when one goes into a river a second time. Heraclitus's view also interestingly suggests that even if the body of water were not a river, and therefore not moving, the second time you stepped into it, *you* would have changed. Heraclitus held that fire is the original element, and he used his concept of "flux" (the flow previously mentioned) to argue that fire condenses into water, Earth melts and produces water, and water in turn produces air and fire. This view can be said to be one of *process*, or a changing substance, in contrast to that of Parmenides.

Empedocles (490–430 BCE) asserted that there are four original elements and that everything comes about through their combination. He perhaps held as his most comprehensive view of the universe that chaos will ultimately prevail.

Anaxagoras (500–428 BCE) discovered that the moon does not shine by its own light but receives it from the sun, thereby being able to explain eclipses correctly. His most comprehensive view of the universe is that design is the more prevailing explanation, when compared to chaos.

These four concepts—constancy, process, chaos, and design—can be seen as forerunners to several features of contemporary physical and astrophysical theories about the nature of the universe and its underlying structure. They have also played a very significant role in the development of physical and biological explanations and models of natural processes throughout history. The contrast between the views of Parmenides and Heraclitus is particularly important in the development of ideas about motion that led to the scientific revolution of the seventeenth century, specifically as it relates to the application of mathematics to describe natural phenomena, as will be demonstrated later.

Democritus (460–360 BCE) proposed the idea of indivisible atoms as the basic constituents of all matter. All of nature can be understood by the interactions of the atoms and the void that separates them. Democritus can be considered the founder of the philosophy of *materialism*, according to which all that exists is due to the interactions of the atoms across the void and nothing more. This idea has remained historically influential and was incorporated into the modern ideas about matter beginning in the eighteenth century.[6]

The Period of Plato and Aristotle (Fourth Century BCE)

The period of Plato (427–347 BCE) and Aristotle (384–322 BCE) represents perhaps the most mature stage of Greek thought and can serve as the basis for our subsequent discussion of how Greek knowledge has shaped the history of ideas in the West, which of course includes the development of science. The contrast between these two individual views on nature can be seen in their incorporation of the ideas entertained and debated by the pre-Socratic philosophers. It is interesting that we use Socrates (469–399 BCE) as a decisive figure in separating Greek thought from an emerging to a mature state since there are no known writings attributed to him. Most, if not all, of what we know about him is provided by Plato, but Socrates' influence on many ideas that are attributed to Plato appears undeniable. One can infer this since of the many characters that Plato uses in his dialogues, Socrates plays a very special role as the provider of many important arguments, among them that for the immortality of the soul in the *Phaedo*.

For Plato, the ultimate structure of reality is to be obtained through deductive reasoning about abstract ideas (forms) that constitute the basis for all knowledge. Once general principles about abstract ideas are established, we can then see how specific instances are manifested by concrete experiences.[7] Plato's Academy became famous for its adherence to strict mathematical reasoning, and he proposed the clearest challenge to thinkers at that time to provide a model describing the structure of the heavens. This naturally led to several important models proposed as answers, including a consideration of both Earth-centered (geocentric) and sun-centered (heliocentric) views.

It is important to realize that there appears to be an initial rejection of the experimental focus of natural science at his academy due to the perception that manual effort and pragmatic concerns were somehow degrading. This has created a perception that Greek contributions to the development of science were mostly in theoretical aspects and that they appear to have neglected a systematic experimental approach that resulted in many of their conclusions being eventually disproved by subsequent careful observations. This is not entirely accurate, though, since Aristotle's system represents the actual opposite of Plato's and Aristotle's Lyceum emphasized empirical observations as the main source of knowledge about nature. There are nevertheless instances in modern science where Plato's influence is clear, such as in the ideas of symmetry and beauty perceived through mathematics that guide a good deal of theoretical physics research.[8]

Aristotle remains the most important intellectual in antiquity for the development of science. His system is the most comprehensive ever in terms of the organization of observations, their classification, and the exhaustive analysis that he eventually conducted. His influence on Western ideas about almost every aspect of knowledge is truly awesome, and his philosophical system became the greatest source of information and authority on nature that European culture in the Middle Ages would encounter.

Aristotle's contribution to knowledge about nature can be found in most fields of science, ranging in complexity from biology to physics and including many ideas about what have become the fields of psychology and sociology. He also made observations in medicine, meteorology, zoology, and botany. Consider as an example the absolutely concise and elegant way that he is said to have identified the most basic needs of any organism as:

1. the need to stay alive (sustenance), and
2. the need to reproduce.

He subordinates every other organismic need and function to these two. This represents an economy of thought unrivaled in the history of ideas and perhaps unsurpassed by any other natural philosopher. Aristotle's investigations in the physical sciences remained influential for a long time, but encountered many more difficulties than those in the life sciences since the evolution of understanding about the physical world traditionally has been led by discoveries in areas where there is a low level of complexity.[9]

Figure 3.1 represents the relationships among:

1. knowledge about nature expressed in degrees of confidence about what can be found expressed as certainty,
2. the level of complexity of the objects/systems studied, and
3. investigations that cover the full range from the simplest systems found in physics to the most complex found in biology.

The figure shows that, as the complexity of the subject (an object, system, or collection of interacting objects) increases, the level of confidence or degree of certainty in what can be known about it decreases. What has become known as *causality* or cause-effect relations identified in nature appear to have had its origins in Socrates' alleged admission that studying the

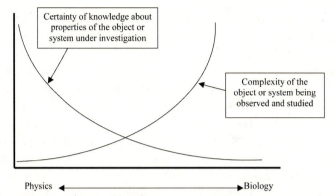

Figure 3.1. Relationship between degrees of knowledge and complexity found in nature. As the complexity of what is observed and studied increases, the level of confidence of what becomes knowledge about it decreases.

behavior of physical systems allows for an easier determination of its causes or, in modern terms, the variables that determine the systems' behavior. This determination becomes progressively more difficult when studying animate objects and living systems, where even the behavior of a simple worm cannot be easily attributed to certain specific causes.

We might admit at this point that the use of the term *certainty* is perhaps too ambiguous in describing the knowledge that can be obtained about nature. The claim made by Plato is that the only type of knowledge that can be considered certain, in the sense of being infallible or not prone to error, is mathematical. Purely deductive reasoning renders knowledge about nature based on observations no longer certain and perhaps not even considered true knowledge.

Aristotle and his European successors in the Middle Ages would agree that empirical knowledge will forever be an attempt to obtain the highest level of confidence in our conclusions.[10] We might therefore, within the confines of the aforementioned correspondence and coherence views about truth, substitute the terms *accuracy* and *precision* for *certainty* and *confidence* in our conclusions about observations. *Accuracy* can be defined as the degree of agreement (correspondence) between what we determine about nature based on observations and reflection, expressed either qualitatively (as a description) or quantitatively (as a measurement), and the actual features or properties as we believe them to exist independent of our efforts. This rather simple distinction between observer and whatever is being observed underwent a dramatic revision in twentieth-century physics. However, we can use it for the purpose of establishing clarity in our discussion. *Precision*, on the other hand, can be defined as the degree of agreement or consistency in our claims (coherence) about nature.

The concept of precision can also be used in figure 3.1 as it relates to a prominent property of scientific knowledge that will be discussed in chapter 6: the principle that a particular strength of scientific theories is not that they can be confirmed as being undeniably true, but that they can be shown to be *false*. The more precise a hypothesis is, the more *falsifiable* it becomes. Conversely, concepts that are rather imprecise or ambiguous are more difficult to falsify. For example, the concept of inertia (the tendency of a mass to resist changes in its state of rest or motion with constant speed) cannot be directly measured, although it can be easily tested. A comparable non-scientific idea would be the concept of freedom, which cannot be measured directly, either, but can nevertheless be seen as a very real human property.

Since we wish to avoid errors in our conclusions, accuracy seems a more desirable goal than precision, at least in measurements in scientific work. Nevertheless, as will be discussed later, science can be said to have been made possible by the implicit assumption of *realism* or the existence of a reality independent of the senses. Therefore, to conclude that knowledge arrived at through sensory experience (including the extensions afforded by our increasingly sophisticated instruments) corresponds to what is *real*, whether we discover it or not, is most likely a metaphysical conclusion, not a scientific one. Consequently, the use of increasing accuracy as correspondence between our knowledge about nature and our ever discovering that independent world as it really is, in the Kantian sense, can be said to involve a good deal of faith.

The Kantian sense consists of the view that we can conceive of the reality of nature based on how we perceive the things whose existence we determine to be real, but that we can never know them as things-in-themselves.

There is a great deal of scholarship on philosophical views held of reality as things-in-themselves, and also of the position that the existence of any properties of the universe regarded as independent of observers is held to be nonsensical. These views, however, are metaphysical, and many scientists often dispense with them by declaring them to be beyond what science, as a way of knowing the universe, was meant to engage in. Other scientists, though, are willing or forced to consider these implications as part of their particular fields of study, where distinctions between physical and metaphysical considerations are often blurred. A particular example is in modern cosmological views of the universe, where the construction of explanatory mechanisms often involves the use of mathematical reasoning and modeling, combined with clearly speculative views about the implications of these explanations. Among these, we can consider the search for extraterrestrial life, the effects of gravity in extreme conditions such as black holes, the preceding and early stages of the observable universe as part of the inflationary theory, and so on.

In contrast to Plato's system (where knowledge of relationships between abstract forms, or universals, can lead to instances of these relationships among concrete objects), Aristotle claims that it is from the relationships found among the objects of observation—the concrete—that one can generalize to abstract or universal properties. In this sense, he clearly anticipates modern scientific thinking.

Plato asserts that only knowledge obtained through mathematical and deductive reasoning can lead to the truth. Sensory knowledge is for him a contradiction in terms, since humans are notoriously prone to err. If we derive any sort of knowledge from empirical investigations of nature, we must accept that it is subject to uncertainty and thus *cannot* lead to the truth.[11]

By being common sense, according to Aristotle, knowledge about nature becomes less certain, and he qualifies his scientific observations with the realization that general laws are only approximations of objective reality. Since, in this view, certain knowledge appears now to be perhaps unattainable, one can only obtain a degree of precision and accuracy to the extent allowed by the subject of study. The role of human error involved in perceptions that are inaccurate—like optical illusions and mirages—combined with the inherent error in using instruments, requires that repeatability provide the best assurance against error in sensory knowledge. This would become the basis for induction and receive considerable attention during the Middle Ages of scholars in Europe.

Aristotle's analyses and conclusions about nature that have been found to be incorrect are the result of his excessive reliance on the use of syllogistic thinking. A *syllogism* (incidentally attributed to him) is a way to tackle any problem where knowledge is sought. One begins with premises (statements) known to be true, and, by strict adherence to the principles of logic, one can deduce or conclude something that must follow and that one didn't know initially.

As an example of deductive reasoning, consider the following argument:

I. To study the nature of science requires deep thinking skills.
II. This book is about studying the nature of science.
III. Therefore, this book requires deep thinking skills.

Analyze the following argument:

　I. All perception is about something being perceived.
　II. I am perceiving that you are confused.
　III. Therefore, you must be confused.

- Is this the only way to know that someone is confused?
- Does the perception correspond to the actual state of being confused?
- Does the argument change if we replace "All" in statement I with "Most"?

The argument seems valid, since the second and third premises follow from the first one—although, as we'll discuss later, the truth of the first premise cannot be demonstrated by logic but only by experience.

The main principles in syllogistic thinking are those of noncontradiction and the "law of the excluded middle." These principles rest on the realization that something cannot be both what it is and what it is not at the same time, thereby excluding a middle position where being and nonbeing coexist. Statements made about anything that can be considered logical can either be true or false, but not both simultaneously.[12] Aristotle found the power of syllogistic thinking too persuasive to allow for detailed observations and further examination in those areas where such an empirical approach might have shown him that it could be otherwise.[13]

Aristotle's ideas and their influence on subsequent views about motion provide a context that can be helpful in understanding the development of modern physical theory, which brought about the scientific revolution of the seventeenth century. Aristotle made a distinction between motion on Earth and motion in the heavens, and he postulated a view to account for an object set in motion and afterward not acted upon by the agent that set it in motion. Both of these ideas were effectively challenged. The first concept was found to be incorrect in the seventeenth century, and the second was severely criticized beginning in the sixth century.[14]

Despite these apparent shortcomings in his perceived understanding of motion in some specific instances, one of Aristotle's most profound insights about nature is his general definition of motion as change, not only in terms of position but also in other processes and properties of objects.[15]

The unique and perhaps most powerful feature of Aristotle's philosophy is its comprehensiveness, and the fact that there are exceptions to every rule was evident to him in his admission that generalizations about natural phenomena work for the most part, but not in every instance. His use of the law of the excluded middle or "golden mean" not only forms the basis for all logical thinking but also serves as a yardstick for appropriate behavior in his view of human relations. This follows from his belief that the greatest activity humans can engage in is in the art of discussion (*polemic*), what he considered "politics" proper or the engagement of the *polis*, the entire civic community. The larger context for Aristotle's cosmological views, his treatment of gravity—the tendency of some objects to fall—and levity—the tendency of some others to rise—is a reflection of an impulse to set things right, to restore balance and proportion, and to return to one's natural and proper state.[16]

This sense of proportion represents the culmination of a very unique view of our relationship to the rest of nature that had been developing in Greek thought. Of particular prominence in this view is the application of the idea of balance and proportion to the concept of measurement, which is seen as coming from within or being an internal property, whereas in our modern view, measurement is a comparison to an external standard, clearly an external property.[17]

Another feature of Aristotle's comprehensive system of knowledge is his view of causation, which provides a context in which one can see the totality of explanation of natural phenomena.[18] He regards the following as the causes of things in nature:

1. The efficient cause (whatever makes the thing)
2. The formal cause (what its form is)
3. The material cause (what the thing is made of)
4. The final cause (what its reason for being is)

The significance of Aristotelian causality lies in the comparison to a particular feature of modern science. It consists of the gradual rejection since the seventeenth century of the last category of causation, namely, the use of the final cause. This is something that will become clear when we look at Galileo's views of nature and their significance for the scientific revolution that followed.

There are a number of other prominent thinkers contemporary with Plato and Aristotle; however, their contributions were in areas other than astronomy and physical science, and their systems were not as comprehensive, so their views on topics such as medical science will be analyzed later. This will be necessary in the study of medieval contributions and the transformation of medical practice in particular.

The Hellenistic Period (300–100 BCE) and Greco-Roman Period (100 BCE–400 CE)

During the Hellenistic period following the expansion of Greek civilization by Alexander, there are a number of important contributions. Theophrastus (c. 372–287 BCE), who was Aristotle's successor at the Lyceum, made extensive contributions to botany, and Strato (c. 335–269 BCE) made significant contributions to physics by correcting some of Aristotle's errors in this field. There are also a number of astronomers associated with the Library at Alexandria who made important contributions to geography and astronomy. Among these were Eratosthenes (c. 275–195 BCE), who was the first to measure the circumference of the Earth; Hipparchus (fl. second century BCE), who introduced the concept of epicycles that would play an enormous role in subsequent models of the universe, and who used trigonometry in his work; Aristarchus (c. 320–250 BCE), who introduced the heliocentric hypothesis, although this had few followers since it requires experimental evidence that was nearly impossible to obtain then; and Claudius Ptolemy (c. 100–170 CE), who provided the most comprehensive astronomical system known from antiquity, which was followed for nearly 1,500 years.

For our purposes, the most important thinker in this period is Archimedes (c. 287–212 BCE), who was perhaps the greatest scientist and engineer from antiquity. His accomplishments are legendary and many—chief among them, his discovery of the principle of buoyancy that is also known as Archimedes' principle. Archimedes' work also represents the best example from antiquity of the use of mathematics in the investigation of nature. That he nearly discovered a mathematical formalism similar to calculus shows that his contributions to the field of mathematics are of the greatest significance.[19]

As part of a historical connection between Greek ideas and scientific views, we can list among the clear instances of an influence of Platonic and Aristotelian ideas on modern science, particularly on modern physics, the following:

- Beauty as analogous to truth in modern theoretical particle physics
- Aristotelian potentialities becoming actualities as part of the current wave function interpretation in quantum mechanics
- Aristotle's "final cause," which, while appearing to have been rejected in modern evolutionary theory, nevertheless figures in theoretical physics as the idea that to know something is to understand its purpose
- The belief that the ultimate structure of the universe can best be described mathematically

Aristotle's idea of something existing potentially, such as a tree existing in the form of an acorn and the acorn eventually turning into the tree, can be seen to play a similar, although more complex, role in the current understanding of subatomic phenomena. As will be explained later, a subatomic particle such as an electron is understood as existing (potentially) in the shape of a probability wave, until an observation or measurement causes it to manifest itself as an actual signal on an instrument.

In concluding our discussion of Greek contributions to knowledge in the context of the development of ideas that will become part of the scientific approach to an understanding of nature, we can summarize some other features that have been shown as being imported from Egypt:

- Thales' inversion of the triangular shape of a pyramid for the purpose of locating ships at sea based on the determination of their distance from the shore
- Pythagoras's use of calculation techniques to be converted into universal mathematical precepts

Pythagoras's recognition that a properly scientific explanation must reduce relationships to universal laws that are mathematically expressed is a direct ancestor of the views of nature in the age of Isaac Newton.

Atomism is one of the most important ideas about nature contributed by the Greeks. Its proponents claim that, at the level of perception, the material world is divisible into fundamental particles that are not further divisible. This idea can be taken as the basis for *reductionism*, an approach to determining the basic constituents of the material world that continues to drive the search for the basic structure of the universe. However, as we'll see later, this approach may be an exercise in futility, since recent developments in the understanding of certain properties of objects and systems called "emergent" appear to indicate that a holistic rather than a reductionist view may be necessary to explain these systems.

Philosophical considerations appear to force us to conclude that a truly fundamental description of the natural world may be unattainable. An analysis of Greek ideas is therefore essential to understand the incredible explanatory power provided by empirical knowledge and reasoning about the natural world, in addition to allowing us to see the limitations that such an approach has.

The current chapter aimed to show the significance of Greek contributions to knowledge about the natural world. The goal is to demonstrate the evolution of the earliest attempts to provide a comprehensive view of nature—which is, after all, the goal of science. A short discussion of some general philosophical definitions was therefore unavoidable in the context of a consideration of different forms of knowledge.

In the next chapter, we will deal with the *legacy* of the Greek contributions, particularly as they were adopted and criticized in subsequent applications of their significant accomplishments in many areas of knowledge.

⁓

Items for Reflection

- What do you think is the main difference between Democritus's concept of atoms and the modern one?
- If we use a pencil as an example of an object to which the Aristotelian "causes" can be applied, how would you go about describing each one?
- What is your view of the popular conundrum: If a tree falls in the forest and there are no means to detect it, is there a sound?

For Further Reading

Chisholm. R. *The Theory of Knowledge*. Englewood Cliffs, NJ: Prentice-Hall, 1966.

Cohen, M., and I. E. Drabkin. *A Source Book in Greek Science*. New York: McGraw-Hill, 1948.

Sambursky, S. *The Physical World of the Greeks*. Princeton, NJ: Princeton University Press, 1987.

CHAPTER FOUR

~

Knowing, Doing, and the Inevitability of Curiosity and Exploration

The Greeks' intellectual contributions were largely the result of two general features of their approach to knowledge: first, their adoption of elements of knowledge—mathematical, geometrical, astronomical, and more—that came from other geographical regions, and second, a rather unique perspective on the way they questioned everything, in terms of methodology. The next phase in our study of the evolution of ideas about nature that led to the emergence of science and its applications results from the Greek distinction between two types of knowledge:

- True knowledge (*epistemë*, from which *epistemology* comes), that is, causal knowledge, or in the Aristotelian sense, *why* a thing is as it is, and
- Knowledge of *how* to do something (*technë*, from which *technology* comes), which implies a sort of knowledge somehow inauthentic.

The Romans became the immediate heirs of the Greek accomplishments, except that they were more interested in the *applications* of Greek ideas than in the ideas themselves. This is not to imply that there weren't great thinkers who advanced the state of knowledge for its own sake, however. Indeed, there are many examples of great accomplishments by Roman civilization in empirical explorations of the natural world.

Lucretius (98–55 BCE) made extensive contributions to the study of matter, further developing the atomic ideas. He also dealt with ideas about energy and held an evolutionary view of the origins of the Earth. Seneca (8 BCE–64 CE) provided detailed descriptions of earthquakes and geography, although his work appears to be almost totally based on Greek ideas. Pliny the Elder (23–79 CE) wrote the important *Natural History* and died tragically at the eruption of Vesuvius while investigating it. Several logical extensions of the applications of Greek ideas led the Romans to their greatest accomplishments, in architecture and engineering.[1] The conflicts resulting from the expansion of the Roman Empire also led to the invention of many mechanical devices for military purposes.

Among the significant Roman discoveries are cement, heating by convection, an understanding of the dependence of water speed on the depth of a pipe, and several features of large-scale buildings based on a revolutionary new way to support structures. The arch—described by Leonardo da Vinci, one of the greatest engineering minds in history, as "a strength springing from two weaknesses"[2]—used as a support is a very clever invention (which probably came from the Arabs) in building large structures. Greek architecture does not show evidence of this knowledge—try finding an ancient Greek building anywhere that doesn't have straight-line design; the classical structures all have columns supporting horizontal beams.

Figure 4.1 shows the advantage of an arch over a beam when used as a support. The diagram at the left shows three beams of stone, two used as supports or columns (A and B) and the third (C) spanning horizontally the space between the other two. The arrows represent the force of gravity on the pieces; the two arrows at the end of the beam are balanced by the supports A and B, so the beam is in equilibrium at the ends. In the middle, the beam is not in equilibrium, and the larger middle arrow represents the pull on the beam by the Earth. The diagram at the right shows that when stone is used as pieces to make an arch, the force of compression between the pieces is

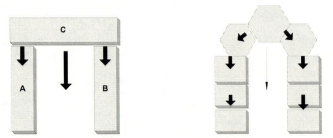

Figure 4.1. Two ways to use stone as support: on the left as the typical post-and-lintel, and on the right as an arch made of several pieces.

much larger than the force of gravity will be on the pieces—particularly the one that sits on top, as shown by the different arrows. If one imagines a very long beam C, then it clearly will be affected more at the middle, whereas if one places many pieces of stone, they will create a very long arch that will avoid the problem.

Why is the arch so much superior to a beam? After all, the beam (due to its straightness) has a more rigid and stronger appearance. This is, in fact, only true when dealing with compression; a column made of stone will be ideal for support, since stone has a high limit of compressional stress.[3] When used as a beam, stone will be affected by its low limit of shear and tension stress, and so the force of gravity at its center of mass will eventually cause it to buckle and collapse. This is clearly avoided by the arch arrangement.

The use of the arch enabled the Romans to build structures such as aqueducts, churches, and bridges with the supports spanning very long distances. Figure 4.2 shows one of the most famous aqueducts, the Pont du Gard in southern France; the lower arches span a width comparable to that of a six-lane highway.[4]

The architectural structures and engineering feats accomplished by the Romans serve as examples of the applications of empirical knowledge to practical situations. However, Roman civilization is also greatly helpful in our consideration of the use of Greek knowledge about ourselves. This is

Figure 4.2.   The Pont du Gard, France, built in the first century CE. *Source:* **Thinkstock**

due to the Romans' development of the most comprehensive treatment of principles of law and civic duty, and their humanistic approach to knowledge. Three intellectuals are particularly important for understanding how knowledge was classified and categorized at the time.[5]

1. Martianus Capella (fourth or fifth century CE) compiled all that was then considered knowledge into the seven "liberal arts": the Trivium ("Three Ways")—grammar, rhetoric, and dialectics—for expressing thought, and the Quadrivium ("Four Ways")—arithmetic, music, geometry, and astronomy—to organize what was known.
2. Boethius (480–524 CE) maintained that it is through the Quadrivium, using the discipline of philosophy, that one is led from the senses to the surer things of intelligence. He became a very important source of knowledge for medieval thinkers.
3. Cassiodorus (488–575 CE) compiled knowledge similarly to Martianus Capella, but in more detail, according to the hierarchy shown in table 4.1.

One of the most significant events in the history of science is the emergence of Christianity and its eventual adoption as the state religion of the Roman Empire by the end of the fourth century. The ideas of Genesis, in particular that of Creation, were seen as compatible with Plato's ideas as expressed in the book *Timaeus*, translated from Greek into Latin in the fourth century, where he explains his cosmological views. This book would become the main source of information about the cosmos in Europe for almost eight hundred years. Aristotle's views, on the other hand, would come to be seen as incompatible with Christianity since he claimed, among other things, that:

Table 4.1. Classification of Knowledge in the Fifth and Sixth Centuries CE

Philosophy	Theoretical (*inspectiva*) "True Knowledge"	Physics (*naturalis*)	
		Mathematics (*doctrinalis*)	Arithmetic
			Music
			Geometry
			Astronomy
		Metaphysics (*divinalis*)	
	Practical (*actualis*) "Applied Knowledge"	Ethics (*moralis*)	
		Economics (*dispensativa*)	
		Politics (*civilis*)	

- Nature exhibits determinism, or an inevitability that would rule out miracles.
- The cosmos is eternal, which appears to rule out the concept of Creation.
- The soul is the organizing principle of the body, but it is to the body as form is to matter and thus cannot be separated, which argues against the soul's immortality.

Thus the general aspects of Aristotle's philosophy were regarded as pagan by Christian thinkers.

The upheaval that resulted from the gradual disintegration of the Roman Empire and the imminent collapse of the complex social structure that had made material existence relatively stable and comfortable also created a general feeling of doom among Christian intellectuals. This naturally led them away from investigating the material world, and toward a concentration instead on the spiritual one. Two leading Latin scholars that adopted critical views about Greek philosophy were Tertullian (155–230), who denounced it as a source of heresy, and St. Augustine (354–430), who accepted it as a useful instrument to attain truth and aid divine illumination.

St. Augustine became the main source of authority for European knowledge about the world for nearly seven hundred years. With his system embracing Plato's theory of ethereal forms as being complementary to the study of spiritual aspects of life according to Christian theology, the study of nature took a real step backward. It is important to emphasize that Augustine's ideas are not to be taken as necessarily hostile toward the study of nature, as the view that Christianity repressed or at the very least hindered progress in understanding nature in the early Middle Ages seems to imply.[6]

What Augustine tried to do is to correctly warn against equating *religious* views, entertained with the help of philosophy, to *empirical* views about the world obtained through sensory experience. If one proclaims the truth of the religious view by using knowledge from nature to support it, Augustine realized that—since empirical knowledge, being dependent on experience, could be shown to be incorrect—this would jeopardize the religious argument by rendering it less transcendental and thus susceptible to what one can experience based on observation.

An example of this is the adoption of a geocentric system, with the Earth at the center of the universe, as the proper cosmological view of the world to support the biblical conclusion that humans are at the center of Creation by having been made in the image of the Creator. This view seems perfectly natural, and the observational evidence for the Earth being at the center of the cosmos had been decisive in rejecting other views, including the helio-centric one where the Earth moves around the sun that had been entertained by some Greek scholars. The geocentric system devised by Claudius Ptolemy explained the observational features of the heavens so well that there simply was no need to question it, especially as it had papal support.

A seemingly innocuous detail about time measurements based on astro-nomical cycles that had been the basis for all calendars since the earliest attempts and the need to keep accurate dates for religious reasons, however, led to a crisis that eventually overturned the prevailing view and thus under-mined the authority of the Christian Church. The successful development, at the Church's request, of an astronomical model that made calendar reform feasible also created an intellectual environment whose culmination led to the scientific revolution of the seventeenth century. This can be seen as the result of most medieval thinkers, who blindly accepted knowledge from authority, having failed to heed Augustine's advice not to equate a religious proposition to its empirical counterpart by the use of philosophy. I hope the reader sees that this is a classic example of an important lesson for those who weigh one type of inquiry at the expense of others, as mentioned in the introduction of the various approaches to obtaining knowledge.

Greek knowledge also took an alternative route to the one leading to medieval Europe through the Latin world. After Alexander the Great's conquest, opportunities for preserving and disseminating Greek knowledge had existed in the Middle East. However, it was after Muhammad in the seventh century, and particularly with the intellectual development pro-vided by some of his successors, that an interest in translations of ancient Greek knowledge about the natural world led to the establishment in the Arabian Peninsula of centers of learning unrivaled anywhere in Europe. With the establishment in Baghdad during the ninth century of the most important institute for translations, most of the ancient Greek knowledge was recovered. Several disciplines were apparently more prominent due to their usefulness. Among these were astronomy, medicine, and mathemat-ics. It is peculiar that, despite an enormous interest in translating and improving upon ancient Greek knowledge (resulting in the Islamic world becoming a leader in the understanding of nature), this phenomenon lasted only about three centuries. There is a great deal of interest among scholars as to the reasons why this happened.

It is clear that in Islam, as in Christianity, some aspects of Aristotelian philosophy, pointed out before, are in direct conflict with the biblical origins that are common to these religions. The idea of a Creator and the revelation of a means by which these religious systems claim that one could understand Creation are incompatible with the empirical component of the knowledge that was translated from the Greek. It appears that the most challenging task for thinkers in both religions became the need to incorporate logic and naturalism, as sources of knowledge explicit in Aristotelian philosophy, into the fundamental teachings of these systems. With the spread of Islam, the knowledge that Arabic scholars inherited from the Greeks naturally was brought to other places—in particular to Europe with the Moorish conquest and domination of southern Spain for almost seven hundred years.

There are many important contributions and contributors from the Arabic world to the fields that were translated from the Greek and that eventually became the modern scientific disciplines as we know them. Consider that in astronomy the names of many stars come from the Arabic, as well as many astronomical terms such as *azimuth*, *zenith*, and *almanac*. Islamic scholars developed navigational tools that are dependent on astronomical observations, including the sextant, quadrant, and astrolabe. Chemistry, which was originated as alchemy (*al-chemi* in Arabic) by the Muslims, comes from their attempts to transmute base metals into gold and silver, and from attempts to prolong human existence by discovering the "elixir of life." The Muslims also adopted and developed the Hindu decimal number system that uses nine numbers and zero or "cipher" (from the Arabic *sifr*, "empty"). Algebra (Arabic *al-jebr*, "the binding") was developed by al-Khwarizmi in the ninth century, from whose name "algorithm" comes, as well as trigonometry ("sine" comes from the Arabic) and the beginnings of analytical geometry. An example from the field of optics will serve to illustrate the depth of Islamic science and the incredible influence of Arabic contributions to the development of several scientific fields.

In linking mathematics with optics in the eleventh century, one of the most brilliant Arabic intellectuals, Ibn al-Haytham (Alhazen), provides perhaps the most comprehensive approach to an explanation of phenomena. He combines ideas from geometry, medicine, physics, cosmology, and biology in his explanation of vision and perception. Alhazen manages to reconcile ancient Greek views on optics that were previously thought to be incompatible. Some thinkers attributed vision to the human eye illuminating the objects seen; in other words, in this view, light emanates from the eye and perception takes place when objects intersect this sort of "radiation." Euclid in particular had used the model of a visual cone to represent how this occurred. Other views held that the light actually originated outside the human eye and was received by it and interpreted it accordingly. A description of Alhazen's explanation is shown in figure 4.3.

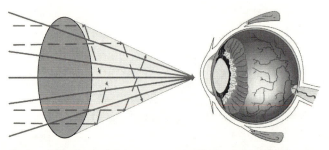

Figure 4.3. A model to represent Alhazen's explanation re-
verses the direction of the rays that make up the visual cone so
that the light comes *into* the eye. The dashed arrows represent
those rays that come in at an angle, so they bounce in a different
direction before getting to the eye. The solid rays represent the
"centric" rays that make up the visual cone by coming into the
eye without having been changed in direction.

The visual cone would naturally extend to the center of the eye so that it
becomes the vertex, and the base of the cone is the visual field.[7] Therefore,
any ray that doesn't strike the eye as a centric ray will not contribute to the
image.

Alhazen's explanation contains elements of the modern treatment in
geometric optics, where technical terms are used to describe the changes in
direction of light rays as either reflection or refraction. In addition, Alhazen
makes use of the concept of radiation as the spreading of rays from points
on objects and their propagation through space and eventual role in perception. This represents a landmark example in the use of geometry to explain
experimentally determined properties of vision. The use of empirical evidence combined with deductive reasoning would play a decisive role in the
resurgence in Europe of an interest in the study of nature in the thirteenth
century due to the impact of thinking like Alhazen's.

Alhazen's influence goes well beyond optical phenomena; his use of geometry on interpreting vision was essential in the development of perspective
painting in the Renaissance, which allowed a precise representation and
reproduction of nature in art and architecture to a degree unavailable before.
An analysis throughout the Middle Ages, beginning with ancient artistic
reproductions of natural scenes and activities, shows the degree of difficulty
encountered in attempting to add depth or relief to depictions on flat sur-
faces. The main idea behind perspective representations is Alhazen's concept
of the *vanishing point*, which is an extension of the use of the vertex of the
visual cone. Figure 4.4 illustrates how the idea of representing depth on a flat
surface—an impossible task since ancient times—was finally accomplished.

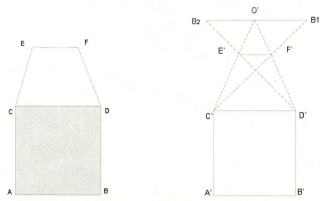

Figure 4.4. The square on the left can be projected so as to create the illusion of depth. The one on the right shows the end result. B1 and B2 are the diagonal vanishing points, and O´ is the principal vanishing point.

With the incorporation of these ideas to add perspective to depictions of nature and descriptions of religious themes, artists in the Renaissance began to express views that were a total departure from earlier styles. Reality and fictional situations could now be shown in the proper scale according to human proportions. In addition to providing the basis for accurate depictions of objects and depth, perspective drawing enabled cartographers to construct accurate maps of the known world, which proved crucial in the momentous geographical discoveries made at the end of the fifteenth century. The application of perspective to maps fixed the distances between places, even if the shapes of the land were distorted by the natural consequence of having to reproduce the spherical shape of the Earth onto a flat surface, pretty much like peeling an orange and finding that the shape of the surface cannot be maintained. Consider the tremendous advantage conferred by having a map with a scale constructed between distances on the map and real distances on the territory the map is meant to describe. Even finding distances at sea becomes possible when a grid, a set of regularly intersecting horizontal and vertical lines, is superimposed on a map.

Figure 4.5 illustrates the distortion of the true size of landmasses that occurs when viewing maps. The distortion is more pronounced for those areas near the poles, as can be seen for Alaska and Greenland. The United States' area is about 4.5 times larger than Greenland, and yet it doesn't look this way on the map. Alaska, which is only 16 percent of the area of the United States, appears much larger than it is by comparison. In fact, the map does not show that the U.S. landmass is almost six times as large as Alaska.

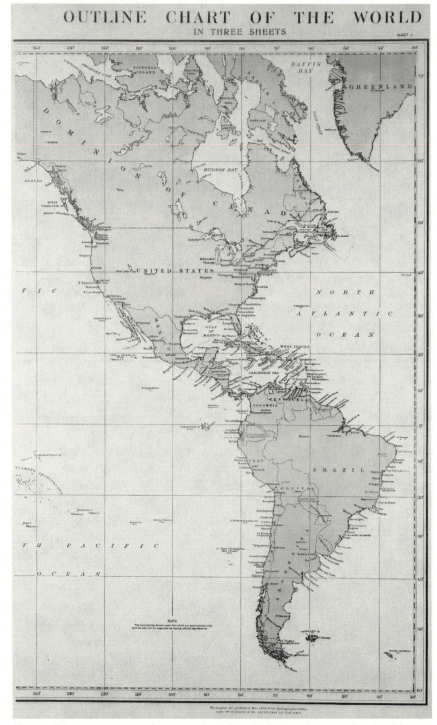

Figure 4.5.   A Mercator projection map of the North American continent would suggest that Alaska and Greenland are much larger landmasses than they really are due to the distortion inherent in representing the part of the Earth's spherical surface on a plane. *Source:* Library of Congress, Prints & Photographs Division, FSA/OWI Collection, [LC-USF345- 007754-ZA]

This brief discussion of the significance of Alhazen's contributions to optics is only meant to illustrate that the application of geometry to explain aspects of perception that had been known since antiquity corresponds to real properties of the human eye, such as the existence of the blind spot. In other words, the eye does have a property, which has the shape of a cone, where its base includes objects that are not visible. Additionally, it is known that Ptolemy and Alhazen both were aware of the fact that viewing distance is a factor in the way we perceive the shape of objects. This is an area that still receives a great deal of experimental attention, because it reveals the extent to which perception (which is a visual effect) can be explained by optical reasoning, a clear precursor of modern scientific thinking.[8]

Another area of important contributions from antiquity is the evolution of the understanding of human anatomy and physiology that gave rise to medical practice. As stated previously, the main difference between medical practice in Babylonian and Egyptian societies and that of the Greeks is the latter's predominantly secular view of disease and their attempts to separate superstition and magic from physical diagnosis and treatment. In this aspect, they owe more to Egyptian than to Babylonian views. It should be noted that Greek medicine did have an early religious aspect to healing that was based on the cult of Asclepius, the god of healing. However, beginning with Hippocrates (460–370 BCE) and his followers, the art of healing became experimental, and disease was viewed as strictly due to natural causes.

Hippocratic medicine attempted to create standards for medical practice with a view of disease as a lack of balance in the body, and treatment as mostly preventive and a restoration of that balance consistent with Aristotle's stance on nature. The observation that many ailments responded to specific treatments such as the use of laxatives, purging, narcotics, and the treatment of wounds did not, in their view, exclude the possible divine origin of disease through natural causes. Despite evidence that dissection of

There is evidence that lenses were used as early as the fourteenth century to correct vision problems like near-sightedness. This was accomplished by the person wearing spectacles or their more modern counterparts, eyeglasses. Both a telescope and a microscope also use lenses, but instead of placing them side by side to correct for vision problems, they are placed one in front of the other at various distances. Since both instruments were not discovered until the seventeenth century, what reasons can you offer as to why it took almost three hundred years for someone to realize this?

the human body had been allowed in earlier times, a particular limitation of Hippocratic medicine based on therapeutic approaches in human anatomy is the absence of dissection, which appears not to have been generally practiced. Nevertheless, several important features of medical knowledge were bequeathed by the Hippocratic writers to the greatest medical authority from antiquity, Galen (130–200 CE).[9] Among these were:

1. Systematic anatomical studies based on the dissection of human corpses by Herophilus and Erasistratus in the third century BCE
2. The discovery of the function of nerves
3. The study of the motion of blood and the function of the heart
4. The understanding of the functional differences between arteries and veins
5. The separation of religious and superstitious elements from the study and treatment of disease
6. The focus on direct observation and cataloguing of clinical findings
7. The significance of the life history of the patient
8. The integration of psychological and physiological aspects in understanding health and disease
9. The welfare of the patient as a moral and civic being as the ultimate goal, beyond physical health

Galen is an important figure because his approach to medicine is part of a comprehensive philosophical view of nature and he is credited with introducing a reductionistic approach to medical practice, where specific organs are identified as the culprits in diagnosis. He relied mainly on the pulse and urine analysis for these purposes. Another important reason for Galen's enormous influence and popularity in the evolution of medical knowledge for almost 1,400 years is his introduction of a teleological (purpose-driven) view in his writings on anatomy and physiology.[10] Some of his empirical findings were challenged and improved upon by the great Arab physician Ibn-Sina (Avicenna) in the eleventh century and by Paracelsus and Andreas Vesallius in the sixteenth century. Nonetheless, this view of health, disease, and healing embedded in a general philosophical disposition continues to animate and influence discussions on whether there is a purpose to the universe and to human behavior in particular.

Galen is also a significant figure in the development of an empirical approach applied to understanding the human body, through his constant appeal to the role of experience in diagnosis. However, Galen's insistence that his disciples study his writings on method, and not rely so much on the authority represented by his accomplishments, would not be heeded by posterity. His conclusions became so authoritative that their use in this manner actually hindered progress in the development of medicine for over a thousand years. Such unquestioning acceptance was actually inconsistent with his approach of disregarding authority in favor of experimental practice.[11]

The role of Galen's work in the development of Western medicine can be used as the background for a discussion of the role of computer simulations in anatomy courses and in the training of medical students with the use of virtual depictions of physiological processes and case analyses. There are differing views on the value of virtual tasks for life science educational purposes, when access to real situations is impractical or seriously limited.

What constitutes a better means to engage prospective medical students in activities dealing with the human body: a task where the student does all the work, or one where most of the aspects that can be considered drudgery are done by technologically aided means? The value of kinesthetic experiences in a general sensory-driven manner as part of hands-on educational opportunities, as opposed to the mostly visual impact of computer simulations on learning tasks, can be used to make Galen's contributions to the role of experience in medical diagnosis relevant.

This chapter has been based on a discussion of the Greek legacy as it manifested itself in two ways: first, its influence on Roman knowledge in general, with a particular emphasis on engineering and architecture as examples of the practicality of scientific knowledge, even if not technically defined as such during that period, and second, the Arab contributions to medieval knowledge, which were absolutely essential to the emergence of science as a distinct way to look at nature.

⁓

Items for Reflection

- Some leading scientists and other scholars believe that the influence of Islam has been detrimental to the growth of scientific knowledge in countries where it is the major religion. However, there are other religious views where standard medical practices such as blood transfusions are forbidden. Do you feel that there are unavoidable conflicts between traditional religious views and modern scientific practices?

- As pointed out in chapter 2, traditional Chinese medicine practices such as acupuncture are taken seriously by many Western medical practitioners. Why do you suppose this is so?

For Further Reading

Hitti, P. K. *History of the Arabs*. New York: Macmillan, 1951.

Lindberg, D. C. *Theories of Vision from al-Kindi to Kepler*. Chicago: University of Chicago Press, 1976.

Lloyd, G. E., ed. *Hippocratic Writings*. London: Harmondsworth, 1978.

O'Leary, D. *How Greek Science Passed to the Arabs*. London: Routledge, 1948.

Sabra, I., trans. *The Optics of Ibn Al-Haytham*, vol. 1. London: Warburg Institute, University of London, 1989.

Smith, M. "Ptolemy's Theory of Visual Perception." *Transactions of the American Philosophical Society* 86, part 2 (1996): 101–2.

Walzer, R., and M. Frede, eds. and trans. *Galen: Three Treatises on the Nature of Science*. Indianapolis: Hackett, 1985.

~

CHAPTER FIVE

From the Transcendent to the Temporal

A Transformative Experience

As discussed in the previous chapter, the Romans and Arabs were the main beneficiaries of the Greek legacy in knowledge of the natural world. Both civilizations contributed many innovations and improvements to this knowledge, mainly by active criticism of the inherited Greek ideas. However, these ideas were also apparently neglected and forgotten during a period of European history in which humanity regressed in its understanding of nature.

The period of history that we are about to discuss, the Middle Ages, is one of the most enigmatic and incredibly interesting since, to our modern view of nature, the views entertained by the great majority of the population in medieval Europe are foreign and somewhat bizarre. In order for us to understand the medieval worldview roughly between the years 500 and 1400, we must suspend judgment from our modern perspective.

It is easy to imagine the sense of doom that must have prevailed among the educated classes—those individuals who, based on their education, were aware of the Greek and Roman achievements and who witnessed the gradual breakdown of the established order beginning in the fifth century in Europe. Those scholars who were influenced by St. Augustine's teachings knew that the spiritual dimension had to be the way out of their experienced precariousness of material existence and temporal uncertainty. What are generally considered the "Dark Ages" includes the Viking invasions and general lack of order that rendered community life intensely local and thus severely hindered the exchange of ideas between distant parts of medieval European geographical areas.[1]

The bulk of the knowledge from antiquity that could have been preserved in Europe resided in monasteries that were isolated both geographically and intellectually from the masses. The religious orders were competing for the proper interpretation of scripture as it impacted on everyday life. Any interest in the study of nature was relegated to an insignificant level since there appeared to be no implicit benefit to engaging in such activities, and the realities of disease and war made contemplation of the human condition an exclusively spiritual affair.

It is only with the expansion of Islam and the translations of Arabic works into Latin (which began in Spain in the tenth century) that the weight of the realization of what the Greeks had accomplished in understanding nature became evident. The translations of most of the corpus of Greek knowledge, combined with their methodology as exemplified by the Aristotelian use of syllogistic thinking, gave rise to the scholastic period. This period provides us with the basis for the development of modern scientific thinking by virtue of the resurgence of an interest in the study of nature, thus giving rise to the empirical approach that has become the hallmark of science.

In addition, we can see the perfect consistency between the study of nature and religious beliefs among its practitioners: *To know the Creator is to understand His works.* In this new intellectual atmosphere, the introduction of those Aristotelian views that dwell on the importance of empirical knowledge shows that some aspects of his philosophy were at variance with certain fundamental Christian teachings, although they could be addressed and perhaps even resolved. This appears to have been the objective of the most brilliant theologians in the three monotheistic religions that have dominated spiritual beliefs in the West.

It is, therefore, not surprising that the originators of the scholastic approach, the use of deductive reasoning (including logic and mathematics) to understand nature as a manifestation of divine creation, were Christian monks who came into possession of that ancient knowledge and used it to justify sacred scripture. There are several important figures in the development of scholastic thinking; however, we shall concentrate on those who were instrumental in developing inductive reasoning—the ability to draw conclusions about nature based on observations and reflection upon their significance within a larger context. That context was, of course, a religious one, where theology and philosophy were clearly separated by those who undertook the task of reconciling the Aristotelian view with the Christian one.

The earliest attempts at a systematic approach were taken as the first universities emerged. Formed by groups of scholars that evolved into an organized establishment, these became the main source of developing, maintaining, and transmitting knowledge in the West. The earliest curriculum included the liberal arts at the undergraduate level, followed by the study of specialized subjects such as law, medicine, and theology at the graduate level.

Two prominent features of Aristotle's philosophical system that constitute the basis of scholastic thinking are the use of logic and the emphasis on naturalistic explanations based upon empirical investigations. Despite Aristotle's objections to the use of mathematics as applied to processes instead of as properties of objects, scholastic thinkers pressed on with their attempts. Famous experiments done in antiquity that involved empirical observations coupled with quantitative determinations—such as Eratosthenes' calculation of the size of the Earth—had been done squarely within the Aristotelian prescribed use of mathematics applied to the proper category, namely, as geometrical properties of objects. The scholastic method departed from this practice by beginning to apply mathematical analysis to processes involving change. However, there were inevitable repercussions of this new way to arrive at knowledge that went beyond methodological discussions. The first of these was a particularly problematic aspect of the application of logic (the most important Aristotelian tool) in a religious context: its use to strengthen theological arguments was also accompanied by efforts to refute them.

The greatest interpreter of Aristotle's philosophy, the Spanish Arab Averroes, or Ibn Rushd (1126–1198), provided the decisive step in the application of logic to knowledge. In doing so, he elevated the use of reason to a level that would eventually become a challenge to religious authority. This led to a massive debate in the thirteenth century as academics such as Peter Abelard (1079–1142) and Siger of Bravant (c. 1220–1284) attempted to distinguish between theology and scripture in their interpretation of biblical writings. These thinkers exposed various interpretations of the Bible as containing inconsistencies and even being contradictory.[2] This naturally undermined religious authority, including papal decrees that at the time were meant to control the use of Aristotelian logic in the emerging universities.

The problem with the use of logic in interpreting sacred scripture was Averroes' conclusion, in his comprehensive analysis of Aristotle's work, that philosophy ought not be used to criticize religion, but at the same time it should not submit to religious authority, either. Consequently, it soon became evident that theology and philosophy needed separation, as the relationship between faith and reason proved to be an uneasy one. The certainty that one could achieve about knowledge in general is compromised if beliefs could be undermined by reasoning. This is an area where a great deal of debate ensued concerning whether belief precedes understanding or the other way around. In this respect, the system developed by St. Thomas Aquinas (c. 1224–1274) appears to be the most satisfactory way to reach a compromise in making Aristotle respectable in the face of Christian orthodoxy. The natural conse-quence of St. Thomas's system is that questions of faith will ultimately depend on convictions held *beyond* what understanding can provide, thus rendering knowledge of ultimate answers about reality less than certain and, therefore, having limits.

The second aspect of Aristotle's philosophical system—one that bears greatly on our quest for an understanding of the evolution of scientific knowledge—is that naturalistic explanations involve the use of induction. The adoption of induction as the basis for empiricism represents an abso-lutely crucial step in the development of science. Induction requires the use of sensory experience based upon repeated observations of nature, which combined with rigorous analysis can provide us with reliable knowledge. This represents a new outlook in the perception of natural phenomena; the context is no longer simply a theological framework. Whereas under the Augustinian worldview everything at the level of perception was typically regarded as a symbol for something religious, this new perspective required an entirely different approach to the quest for knowledge about nature.

The work of two individuals best exemplifies what the scholastic approach incorporated into the study of natural phenomena. The first of these is Roger Bacon (1214–1294), who proclaimed the need for verification of knowledge convictions by means other than those based upon deductive or syllogistic reasoning as the Aristotelian system dictated. Bacon appears to be the first thinker to stress the need to incorporate evidence from all four types of knowledge convictions described in chapter 3 to arrive at knowledge that can be certain from the perspective of the knower.

The beginnings of a systematic use of empirical information as a criterion for knowledge can be traced back to Bacon's *Opus Maius*. In it, he stated that, despite having the assurance of proofs obtained through deductive reasoning such as geometric statements, nothing can be sufficiently known without experience.[3] By "experience," Bacon appears to have meant more than just information provided by the senses, since he held that one needed to appeal to divine illumination in seeking certitude of judgment.

The other significant scholastic intellectual in our discussion is John Duns Scotus (1265–1308), who could rightfully be credited with the re-alization at the time that certitude is possible without the need of divine illumination. He provides the basis for the use of induction as a dependable and justifiable means of arriving at knowledge, thus bringing the Aristote-lian system to bear directly on the study of the natural world to strengthen theological thinking.

According to Duns Scotus's philosophy, a work of reason unaided by faith can use inductive methodology to obtain a form of knowledge about nature. While this is not absolutely certain in the way deductive or mathematical knowledge could be, it is nevertheless viable and useful.

This realization is truly revolutionary, since it provides the way for the third distinctive criterion of scientific knowledge from chapter 3—testability—to become possible for the first time in history. At the same time, it provides us with a unique perspective to see how scientific investigation began as a systematic and methodological inquiry into nature during the thirteenth century. This is a feature that was to evolve into natural philosophy and that would eventually divorce itself from scholastic speculations in the seventeenth century.

Duns Scotus's uncanny realization that one can obtain inductively reliable knowledge from unreliable sources is essential for an understanding of certain assumptions that lie at the core of scientific practice. Among these assumptions are:

- *realism*, the belief that our theories about natural phenomena contain constructs that match real entities and properties possessed by nature
- *determinism*, the belief that there are antecedent conditions which dictate that a thing could not be other than what it is
- *causality*, which in a very general sense is the assumption that every change, or lack thereof, occurs under innumerable and infinitely complex conditions—some of which are such that the change would not have occurred without them, while other conditions have nothing to do with the change[4]

The considerable importance of Duns Scotus's contribution is that he demonstrates that limited observations can suffice to establish the reasonableness of the above assumptions about nature. Two statements, slightly paraphrased, will serve to illustrate his position:

1. Whatever takes place or occurs in many instances by a cause that is not free, is the natural effect of this cause.
2. Even if a person cannot experience every single individual instance, but only a great many, and even if the person does not experience them at all times but only frequently, nevertheless the person, based on these experiences, knows intuitively that it must always be so and in every case.[5]

These claims serve as the basis for an investigation of nature where our findings can yield reliable knowledge even if we cannot observe every instance and if we are not present to confirm the predicted outcomes.

Duns Scotus claims that if we should be misled by the appearance of something that is not in reality taking place, we can still rely on sensory experience to arrive at what is real about our observations. An example that was commonly used by scholastic thinkers was that of a straight piece of wood that, when partly submerged in water, appears to be broken. If the visual perception that the wooden object looks broken is incorrect, simply touching it would resolve the matter as the sense of touch will reveal that it isn't broken.

The systematic observation and reflection upon empirical information is an entirely new way to look at nature. Scholars arrived at such conclusions by what they called an argument *quia* (reasoning from effect to cause) based on limited observations, as opposed to an argument *propter quid* (reasoning from essence to characteristic), demonstrating an effect from a known cause that would require observations of every possible instance. Although the context of this new way of seeking knowledge is still theological, the role played by natural observations necessitates that, for our conclusions to be true, they must match reality as it is assumed to exist independently of our perceptions. Nature, from this point onward, must be studied by giving priority to the evidence provided by our investigative tools.

Qualitative and quantitative determinations about natural phenomena depend on empirical verification; otherwise, they are not to be entertained as anything but figments of our imagination. In other words, detailed observations followed by rigorous analysis of nature can constitute experimentation by taking the form of a measurement. What is measured can either be expressed as the magnitude of a quantity or as the substantiation of a qualitative conclusion.[6] This methodology can be legitimately taken as the beginning of scientific investigation in the modern sense.

It is important to clarify that, while determinism implies necessity, causality does not. Since inductive knowledge is made possible by the observed regularity of natural phenomena, the conclusions reached by Duns Scotus imply that we decide by the criterion of "not free" what is "natural" in terms of cause and effect. Chaotic or unpredictable behavior in nature does not necessarily rule out a cause, but it certainly makes its determination much more difficult,

---

Some scholars have claimed that the beginning of the scientific revolution actually goes back to the late fourteenth century, when Aristotle's works were condemned by the Bishop of Paris as heretical. Why should this be taken as the earliest attempt to break free of the knowledge acquired from antiquity? And why should this have helped the development of science?

even perhaps rendering it impossible. Therefore, we can say that phenomena observed under the criterion of causality arrived at inductively, combined with our theories to explain them, suggest that whatever we conclude the "laws" of nature to be, such as those governing gravitation or genetics, they are not *necessary*. In other words, natural phenomena can be observed and interpreted in more than one way unless we stipulate certain conditions.

This is a reason why the laws that are said to apply in various scientific areas of study have constraints. Examples include:

- Boyle's law, where the pressure and volume of an ideal gas exhibit the relationship expressed by the equation PV = constant (if the temperature is kept constant)
- Newton's laws applying under frictionless conditions (if the force of friction is either constant or negligible)
- Conservation of energy and momentum under the absence of external forces

The equations that describe phenomena generally require the application of so-called boundary conditions to account for the special circumstances under which they apply. One can manipulate objects and processes by isolating them, or taking them out of their environment as best as possible, to induce other processes that are claimed to be regulated in the sense introduced by Duns Scotus as not being free. Observation and manipulation of natural phenomena would continue to be seen as separate procedures or methods until the advent of modern subatomic physics, where a prominent view holds that the very act of observation alters what is being observed.

If the discovered laws of nature become necessary only when one imposes conditions so that all those factors that could produce a different outcome are effectively controlled, then it follows that *contingency*—the opposite of necessity—is what ensues, since one cannot possibly take into account every possible cause. In other words, the necessity of causal laws is never absolute,[7] since the outcome could always be otherwise. Empirical explanations of temporal events are required because we are in principle unable to trace all the intricate links of causal efficacy that make any given event a necessary and inevitable consequence of a given cause. To this extent, it is entirely feasible that in explaining natural phenomena that are chaotic or inherently unpredictable, even scientific explanations could be superseded by accounts that can take into consideration outcomes that don't depend on conditions imposed to ensure regularity, as our current understanding of the behavior of natural phenomena seems to require.

It is nevertheless remarkable that Duns Scotus made a strong case for the reasonableness of empirical knowledge by realizing that what is necessary and essential about any contingent fact is its *possibility*, since one cannot always infer actuality from possibility. Yet the converse inference is universally valid. This represents an enormously important step in humanity's ability to abstract from incredibly complex situations those features that enable one to undertake a systematic and methodological study of natural phenomena. An acceptance of the possibility of various interpretational schemes to express the laws of physics, in particular, remains an essential component of scientific thinking.[8]

Our discussion of the origins of empiricism and the use of inductive knowledge as one of the most powerful aspects of scientific investigation provides the context in which to understand their prominence as explanatory tools, and their importance in the development of scientific literacy. The fact that there always can be several interpretations of an experimental result will be used as part of the philosophical component of such a context that we will discuss in a later chapter. At this point, however, we must make explicit the pedagogical implications of an epistemologically important feature of students' understanding of empirical findings.

There are a significant number of studies which demonstrate that students possess a view of the nature of science and scientific knowledge that is progressive in structure. Students begin with a very simplistic notion of what constitutes scientific evidence and how it is used, and they gradually develop an understanding of the complexity of the relationship between hypotheses and theories and of the tentative nature of scientific knowledge.[9] At the beginning stages, students don't differentiate between scientific ideas and the evidence used to support them, which is clearly related to the use of data. They also appear to have a linear view that essentially regards hypotheses as becoming theories upon repeated empirical confirmation.

A demonstration of the tentative nature of scientific knowledge will be illustrated in a later chapter using as an example the concepts of increased precision and accuracy in measurements. However, the discussion in this chapter of the beginnings of the use of inductive knowledge, along with the assumptions made about its validity, is relevant to a consideration of certain pedagogical measures. These must be designed to address the need for students to understand that

- theories can be right or wrong depending on the evidence that either supports or challenges them, and

- well-tested hypotheses can gradually lead to theories, but theories in turn can influence what scientists consider testable in the first place.

A thorough discussion of the emergence of inductive knowledge based on limited observations as presented in this chapter can provide teachers with opportunities to engage students in the development of critical thinking skills. For instance, many students are unable to differentiate between predictions, observations, and inferences. To engage them in activities where these three process skills can be effectively integrated provides opportunities to discuss the role of theories and hypotheses (while predicting and inferring), and the extrapolations that can be made to larger settings based on limited but representative observations.

The high Middle Ages are typically not included in discussions of the development of empiricism and scientific thinking, yet they represent perhaps the most fertile period of attempts to investigate nature before the advent of the scientific revolution of the seventeenth century. The discussions of scholasticism are often restricted to strictly religious or philosophical settings; its impact on the development of scientific thinking and knowledge is either ignored or neglected. It is difficult to believe that a distinct period of history could have begun dominated by superstitious and mythical views of the world, with no room for a detailed investigation of natural phenomena under their own right, and have ended with an accommodation of the study of nature in harmony with a predominantly religious view of life.

In this chapter, the scholastic period has been used as an example of the harmony that can exist between the spiritual and the material accounts of reality. The beginnings of empiricism and the use of inductive knowledge to investigate nature have been illustrated. One of the main objectives was to show the reader that the use of logic led medieval Europe to adopt a perspective on nature that became irreversible and that led to the scientific revolution.

⌢

Items for Reflection

- Why do you think scholars commonly refer to a period of medieval European history as the Dark Ages?

- If the Aristotelian system enabled thinkers during the Middle Ages to explore the natural world that was believed to have been God's creation, why would it be considered dangerous from a religious point of view?

For Further Reading

Funkenstein, A. *Theology and the Scientific Imagination from the Middle Ages to the Seventeenth Century.* Princeton, NJ: Princeton University Press, 1986.

Murray, A. *Reason and Society in the Middle Ages.* Oxford, England: Clarendon Press, 1978.

Normore, C. "Duns Scotus's Modal Theory." In *The Cambridge Companion to Duns Scotus*, ed. T. Williams, 129–60. Cambridge: Cambridge University Press, 2003.

Ross, J. F., and T. Bates. "Duns Scotus on Natural Theology." In *The Cambridge Companion to Duns Scotus*, ed. T. Williams, 193–237. Cambridge: Cambridge University Press, 2003.

Wolter, A. B. *The Philosophical Theology of John Duns Scotus.* Ed. M. M. Adams. Ithaca, NY: Cornell University Press, 1990.

CHAPTER SIX

⁓

From Qualities to Quantities

The Mathematization of Nature

The previous chapter detailed the realization by scholastic thinkers that inductive knowledge can provide reliable knowledge of natural events. However, this was only part of their contribution. Their philosophical deliberations led to another profound change in the way that knowledge of the properties of objects was accepted. The impact of an understanding of natural phenomena on every aspect of human knowledge as exemplified by science resulted from the inevitable application of *mathematics* to processes.

Greek approaches to the study of nature under the influence of Aristotle held that mathematics can be applied to an understanding of nature, but only as a property of objects. The determination of the size of the Earth by Eratosthenes serves to illustrate the value of applying geometry and mathematical reasoning to determine specific features of an object such as our planet. Appendix A illustrates the use of mathematics to find the circumference of the Earth as an activity designed to replicate Eratosthenes' important finding. However, the use of geometry and mathematics in instances other than to describe the properties of an object—such as understanding changes and processes—was considered by Aristotle as a category mistake, like confusing apples with oranges. But why should mathematics apply only to objects and not to processes?

Mathematical objects were regarded by Aristotle as an abstraction from physical objects; consequently, quality and quantity as properties were considered different categories. For example, an object possessing properties that can be demonstrated mathematically and measured quantitatively, such as volume or weight, also possesses another property, density, that cannot be directly measured but *can be* determined from the relationship between its mass (obtained from its weight) and its volume. In this sense, we can say that an object's density is an abstraction from its measured mass and volume. Should any of these properties change, they can be determined and measured at every stage. But how do we measure the *process* by which these changes take place?

It appears that, based on Ockham's principle of parsimony, it is imperative to say that an object's change in density is nothing but a reflection of changes in its mass and volume. While we may use the term *density* as an abstraction, there is nothing more in actuality arising from the density changes in an object than those already mentioned.

The identification of the process of change of anything in an object with a different property from those that are actually changing has been a source of controversy and dispute among philosophers ever since the debate between Parmenides and Heraclitus. Additionally, attributing mathematical properties to such processes was not considered appropriate under mainstream Greek thought. An exception to this approach in antiquity had been Archimedes' discovery of buoyancy (the ability of a fluid to push on an object placed in it), which had been accomplished through the use of mathematical reasoning. In fact, Archimedes is known to have been very effective in using geometry and mathematical methods to study and determine properties of nature,[1] and he is believed to have nearly arrived at a discovery of analytical geometry and the calculus.[2]

The break with the Aristotelian position concerning the application of mathematics to the study of natural phenomena came during the fourteenth century with the success of several academics at Oxford and Paris in quantifying change. While applications of mathematics to other areas in antiquity had encountered setbacks, such as with the discovery of irrational numbers, this newly found way to bridge the gap between quantity and quality served to encourage thinkers to exploit the potential that mathematics seemed to have for an understanding of nature.

The ability to measure qualitative as well as quantitative properties of nature was obtained theoretically by the rejection among scholars of the Aristotelian category distinction, claiming that he had used it only as a definition. Methodologically, it was accomplished through the use of a combination of the *intensity of a quality* and the *magnitude of a quantity*. The significance of the Oxford scholars' work for the eventual development of the modern view of motion is to be found in the so-called Merton rule, which was a result of the work of a group of intellectuals at Merton College, Oxford.

As illustrated in figure 6.1, this revolutionary new way of looking at motion, based on a technique for dealing with philosophical problems, paved the way for the eventual proper understanding of motion.

While the technique originated at Oxford, it was later followed and expanded at the University of Paris; the group of individuals responsible for this accomplishment has become known as the "Calculatores."[3] The extension of the applications of the methodology by the Parisian academic Nicole Oresme allowed for the first time a transition in the Aristotelian types of change from a qualitative to a quantitative treatment.

Consider the advantage obtained by using the concepts of "intensive" and "extensive" to represent changes in a quality as demonstrated in figure 6.1. The horizontal lines represent the extension of the quality in the object, while the vertical lines represent the intensity of the quality at a given point. What had been used initially to treat motion strictly in terms of speed was enhanced by Oresme to treat changes in other properties of an object, such as heat distribution.

The mean-speed theorem discovered by the Merton scholars that eventually became a Galilean fundamental axiom of kinematics is shown in figure 6.1a. Simply stated, it says that, in the same amount of time, an object moving with a uniformly changing speed or accelerated motion will travel the same distance as if it were moving with a uniform speed equal to its mean or average value. Oresme's contribution stems from his realization that a quantity of a quality, expressed as the product of an extension multiplied by an intensity, has a physical significance. As shown in figure 6.1a, the proof of

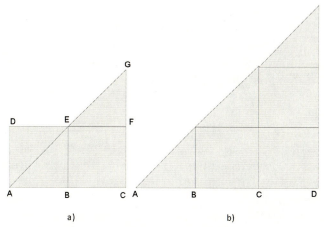

Figure 6.1. **(a) Merton Rule. (b) Incremental changes in distance as an object undergoes a constant change in speed.**

the Merton rule uses the fact that the areas of rectangle DFAC and right triangle AGC are equal. If the extension represents the time, and the intensity represents the speed, then their product as part of the areas of the rectangle and triangle represents the distance. As shown in figure 6.1b, after time intervals AB, AC, and AD, an object having a speed that begins at zero at A and ends with the value represented by the perpendicular at point D will have traveled distances of 1, 3, and 5 units, respectively, corresponding to the areas of the triangles and rectangles included. Galileo's discovery of the proportionality between velocity (taking speed and direction into account) and time follows from this. Galileo's interpretation of the properties of falling bodies, particularly his discovery of the constant acceleration produced by the Earth on all objects near its surface, represents an experimental instance of the first systematic use of mathematics to account for motion.

If there had been apprehension about using mathematics to describe what nature does, with Galileo (1564–1642) there is no longer any doubt that it is through quantitative information that the secrets of the universe will be revealed. Appendix A contains as an illustration two activities that use mathematics to describe the changes in an object's property—its motion.

Even in the case of qualitative information, Galileo made a clear distinction between primary qualities of objects—those essential to provide a measurable quantity of an object's properties, such as extension (length, width, depth) and weight—and those considered secondary by virtue of their interactive nature with observers such as color, taste, texture, and odor. These latter properties depend on our modes of perception, rather than on being real essences of matter.[4] Because these modes of perception are accompanied by the mental processes associated with their necessary internal representation, they lead to phenomena that include consciousness and other features we attribute to human behavior such as ethical values, emotions, and even artistic sensibilities and creativity. Could this have been the beginning of the breakdown of communication between the sciences and the humanities, so clearly formulated by C. P. Snow as the "two cultures" in the middle of the twentieth century?[5]

Galileo's distinction between primary or quantifiable phenomena and those that involve mental activity forms the basis for the perceived objectivity of scientific knowledge since the seventeenth century. This objectivity also includes the clear separation between observers and the objects being observed—another distinction that would persist until the formulation of quantum mechanics early in the twentieth century.

Despite the need to revise our understanding at the microscopic level of the role of the observer in any experiment, observations and the interpretation of experimental data continue to have an ontological difference that can be traced to the distinction between primary and secondary qualities. What gives the primary qualities a superior epistemological status, other than an assumption made to facilitate measurement? The support provided by the enormous success of Galileo's successor, Isaac Newton (1643–1727), in his efforts to unify phenomena at the terrestrial and celestial levels, naturally convinced everyone that Galileo had taken the correct approach.

With Newton, the application of mathematics to the study of natural phenomena takes on a new meaning. His use of modeling to calculate the values of the quantities predicted by his theory of gravitation represents the incorporation of theoretical determinations into a model that could be verified experimentally. An example is his calculation of the moon's orbit based on his gravitation formula, followed by comparison with measurements of its positions. His discovery of the calculus and its application as a means to determine infinitesimal changes revolutionized the way processes could be analyzed. With calculus, the identification of variables that could stand for just about any property of nature—position, speed, temperature, and so on—made prediction a distinctive feature of the application of mathematics to natural phenomena. In fact, Edmund Halley's prediction of the period of revolution of the eponymous comet based on Newtonian theory allowed humanity for the first time to confidently explore the outer reaches of the universe. It also showed European thinkers just how powerful mathematics could be in helping us understand nature. The impact of Newtonian mechanics on seventeenth-century society is, indeed, comparable to what could be called the Aristotelian revolution during the high Middle Ages—the European "discovery" of Aristotle's works and their influence on every aspect of knowledge.

The success of the use of mathematics in describing nature as exemplified by Newton's many accomplishments can be seen in the unification of terrestrial and celestial motion through his theory of gravitation, in his development of a version of calculus, and in his consolidation of previous findings into three comprehensive laws of motion. From Newton's perspective, mathematics clearly provides the means to understand God's creation. To know the Creator is to understand his works.

It would be beyond the scope of this text to explore the relationship between the theological and scientific views and beliefs of individuals like Galileo and Newton. After all, they represent the modern way to look at nature with a tacit acknowledgment on their part that there was no incompatibility between religious beliefs and scientific practice. An important, although not generally known, example of the influence of a theological perspective on scientific accomplishments can be found in the work of a great contemporary of Newton, Robert Boyle.[6]

The continued success of the Newtonian synthesis during the eighteenth and nineteenth centuries appears to have provided support for a materialistic view of the universe as the most scientifically compelling. The emergence of the Darwinian account of evolution as the scientifically accepted view of human origins, as opposed to the idea of creation that had been previously held, appears to have widened the gap between faith and reason, as epitomized by the view that religious beliefs and scientific knowledge are irreconcilable.

Scientific knowledge has progressed at such a pace that, during the last three hundred years, the empirical evidence for an understanding of the universe with the use of mathematics has mounted to such a degree that metaphysical features of scientific practice are seldom questioned among most practitioners. These features are evident in several main aspects of scientific work:

- The use of Ockham's razor as a deciding factor in choosing between hypotheses
- The existence of more than one interpretation of data and phenomena
- The assumptions made about nature being either orderly or chaotic
- The assumption of causality based on determinism

I believe this is an area where misconceptions about the perceived incompatibility between science and spiritual beliefs exist. Any statement based on scientific evidence is, by definition, incomplete and subject to revision. Additionally, metaphysical assertions made about the universe that are based on scientific results, but where the interpretation of data leads to claims that go *beyond* the data, exceed the epistemic authority granted to science on the strength of its theoretical predictions and the validity of its empirical findings and claims.

An example is the attribution of an independent existence to those properties of nature that scientific instruments provide, such as the physical properties that constitute subatomic phenomena, unless one claims that what instruments provide is all there is to such phenomena. This is particularly relevant in light of the accepted view that scientific findings appear to play a fundamental role in all forms of human inquiry. While scientific findings are based on research that involves theoretical as well as experimental techniques, it is worthwhile clarifying what scientific research means. Its definition as a systematic and rigorous way to study nature to ascertain principles and laws includes two basic types of research: *nomological*, based on the regularity exhibited by nature that allows for repeatability, and *historical*, where one studies events and processes that may have occurred only once, or a limited number of times, thus requiring a considerable amount of reconstructive speculation.

Fields such as astronomy, geology, and evolutionary biology, despite their unitary explanatory power, involve a good deal of reconstructions of past events. As such, they may lack the rigor and confidence in the findings afforded by fields where the regularity of nature permits repeated verification of hypotheses and predictions. In such cases, one has to rely on the expected ways that nature has behaved, or will behave, based on presently observed characteristics. This expectation has a metaphysical aspect by virtue of the assumptions made about how the data obtained were generated, and how the processes observed have come about.

Evolution, for instance, seems not to comply with Ockham's razor, since adaptability requires an inevitable differentiation of the structure of an organism. This necessarily leads to the need for an integration of function among the various components of the organism. Such integration becomes more difficult as complexity arises, which implies that successful adaptation demands a harmonious interaction among elements of a complex organism, and this presents many opportunities for malfunction following errors. An analogy can be made with the solution to an algebraic problem, where the required steps may inherently magnify the chances of error in the process.

Nomological research presents the most dependable opportunities to test our theories and hypotheses by allowing for testability, observability, reproducibility, and falsifiability—all distinctive features of scientific practice since the seventeenth century. However, all these characteristics exist to permit determinations of causality. The most basic function of scientific knowledge since the establishment of the earliest scientific societies has been best expressed in its utilitarian way by Francis Bacon (1561–1626), the "prophet" of science: "The end of our foundation is the knowledge of causes, and secret motions of things; and the enlarging of the bounds of human Empire, to the effecting of all things possible."[7]

Causation requires the identification of a cause and an effect. Whether we consider objects, substances, or processes as the *causes*, effects are expected to follow. This is especially true given the acceptance of the principle of induction as proposed by Duns Scotus, where controlled conditions enable what we consider natural effects to take place. This is certainly achievable in nomological research, where controlled, experimental conditions enable repetitive demonstrations of causality to be evident. However, causal explanations involve inferences as well as observations. When inferences are made based on observations that can be repeated under controlled experimental conditions, the metaphysical aspects of scientific work appear minimal due to the repeatability aspects that allow the assumptions made about indirectly observable properties to be immediately tested.

In historical research, on the other hand, inferences often need to be made based on observations of effects whose proposed causes are removed sometimes by considerable time spans, or the assumed causal links are tenuous due to significantly large intervening steps. In this case, inferences are clearly made based on many assumptions that cannot be directly tested. Nevertheless, regardless of whether causal explanations can be offered reliably or tentatively, inductive reasoning has been severely handicapped as a criterion for knowledge since David Hume (1711–1776) in the eighteenth century effectively demonstrated its logical shortcomings.[8] It is ironic that a form of knowledge that has been instrumental in providing science with one of its most powerful tools should have been introduced in the thirteenth century following the strict application of logical principles to the study of nature, and then be found wanting on logical grounds five hundred years later! The significance of the problem of induction lies in what it says about experience, the criterion used by Roger Bacon and the other scholastic thinkers to strengthen knowledge claims.

As Hume pointed out, the fact that an effect would not follow a given cause as part of a regularity required for natural laws to be obeyed is contradicted only by experience, not by conceiving or imagining it. In other words, it isn't illogical or absurd. Furthermore, Hume's criticism appears to render knowledge dependent on experience in general. Stated differently, if knowledge is determined by experience—whether in the form of intuition, reflection, reasoning, or sensory information—can it also be limited by it? Is it possible that since human knowledge is limited, there could be phenomena that we cannot know since they can't be experienced?

If the answer is in the negative, then scientific realism becomes untenable, since it would appear that we, in fact, dictate the nature of reality by subjecting what can be known to what we can experience, rendering what cannot be known about the universe as essentially nonexistent—a far cry from the assumption that there is an independently existing reality that our theories progressively enable us to discover. If the answer is in the affirmative, then realism is upheld, but the epistemic authority of scientific knowledge is undermined in its metaphysical aspirations. Science then cannot answer all questions that can be asked about reality because its tools can enable us to discover only what is empirically verifiable and that can in principle be measured, and measurements are restricted to what instruments are designed to do.

Another aspect of scientific knowledge that has been prominent since the seventeenth century stems from Galileo's reduction of the properties of objects and processes to primary qualities, which are, in principle, extended and thus can be measured. It follows that secondary qualities are more complex, and they can confound the attempts to simplify the study of nature. The ability to introduce controlled, experimental conditions where factors such as friction, air resistance, or constant temperature and pressure can be isolated enables solutions to a given problem where simplicity precedes complexity. No matter how complex a system, it has been standard scientific practice to regard *reductionism* (the ability to break down the system's components into their basic constituents) as the key to finding the solutions to stated problems. Once these limited-case solutions are found, it is possible to extrapolate from the simple situations to the more complicated ones. Solutions to motion problems in several dimensions are usually accomplished by solving the equations in one dimension and then tackling the others. The motion of a projectile, for example, can be described by the same type of equation, but with different conditions for each dimension—in this case, for the vertical and the horizontal components of the motion.

Despite the obvious success of reductionism in most scientific fields, there are some areas where complexity requires an approach in which certain properties of a system are regarded as "emergent," resulting from collective interactions among components that are inherently impossible to analyze individually. In addition, reductionism commits one to a methodological strategy wherein the basic constituents are assumed to be capable of being found. This has certainly been the approach to understanding matter ever since the atomist philosophers. Democritus's view held that atoms, as the basic building blocks, are indivisible, and so at the level of perception, all matter can be said to be composed of them. However, modern atomic theory

---

As an example of the use of induction, consider the following question: Does the fact that the sun "rises" every morning constitute a guarantee that it will do so tomorrow?

has progressively found that the particles considered fundamental, the basic constituents of matter at a given stage, are eventually found to be divisible at smaller scales as the experimental techniques improve in accuracy.

The basic problem with reductionism is that for any object to be the basic constituent of all matter, it must be truly indivisible. Any object that has extension, like a line, no matter how short, can be divided. In fact, a mathematical property of a line is that it is made up of an infinite number of points. So it appears that the only indivisible object would have to be a point. But following the definition of a point as not possessing any extension (or in a more sophisticated version in two dimensions, a circle whose radius becomes zero), an object can be a point if and only if it *is not extended*. How can this be? If the basic constituents of matter are not extended, they are useless as building blocks. In the modern physical understanding of space and time, for an object to lack extension implies that it lacks dimensionality. Since the relativistic interpretation of space and time is as a continuum, a lack of dimensionality requires that such an object be dimensionless not only in space coordinates but also in the time coordinate. No time dimension translates into the object never existing at all!

The obvious success in the practice of reductionism in scientific work is particularly exemplified by many of its technological applications, such as the miniaturization of electronic components and devices, and the advantages this offers for exploration—leading to such practical applications as those in medicine, telecommunications, forensic science, and data acquisition and management, to name but a few. In general, reductionism has enabled fields that are inherently interdisciplinary and dependent on multivariable analysis, to isolate explicit areas of research and concentrate on investigating phenomena at a greatly reduced scale but with a magnified scope. Neurobiological findings about human and animal behavior such as perception, cognition, and a host of anatomical and physiological properties are currently understood in terms of brain function and features. The inevitable reduction of complex phenomena to brain function, in this case, seems compelling to most researchers, since it simplifies their investigation.

The use of reductionism will inexorably lead to ever smaller areas being investigated, with the intent of finding the underlying causes of the observed phenomena at the larger ones. An implicit assumption among some leading scientists is that an explanation will not be fundamental if it can be expressed in terms of a "deeper" one, or one from which it follows in increasing complexity.[9] Nonetheless, other investigators have asserted that reductionism is untenable, as demonstrated in the most basic of the sciences, physics.[10] The

A good demonstration of the limits of reductionism is provided by looking at a newspaper photograph with a magnifying lens. As you look at the photograph first without the lens and then with it, what do you notice?

question is: How deep can we go? If the depth is such that we need to invoke fundamental entities in the sense defined above, have we reached the limit?

It appears that having reached a level of description and understanding that cannot possibly be made of fundamental points or similar entities, one would either declare victory or accept defeat, depending on one's perspective.

The above considerations illustrate some of the metaphysical difficulties accompanying our modern understanding of several features of the universe that have arisen due to the incremental success in describing and explaining nature scientifically. Some of these difficulties have been part of the evolution of scientific knowledge from natural philosophy to the prominent role it displays in modern life. Others are simply the inevitable outcome of the increasingly obvious power that the type of knowledge envisioned by Francis Bacon has conveyed upon humanity. While some practicing scientists may acknowledge these issues, the majority are certainly able to dispense with such intellectual "niceties" and continue unhindered in their pursuit of the answers that scientific methodology continually hints at.

Many people still seem to entertain superstitious and supernatural beliefs that were prevalent before the naturalistic explanations made possible by science. Yet, there is an odd corollary to this. There seems to exist *within the scientific community* the desire to believe that it is science that can provide the ultimate answers to all of mankind's most profound questions. This shows, if nothing else, how deeply engrained the "need to know" has become in the fabric of modern thought.

In this chapter, the quintessentially defining characteristic of scientific knowledge has been introduced and explained using the evolving understanding of motion as an example. This allows the reader to see that it was the efforts to understand motion properties that brought about the scientific revolution. The conviction is that nature can ultimately yield its secrets through mathematical representations and with the use of models. However, there is also the need to highlight the limitations inherent in the practice of one of the most salient features of scientific explanations: reductionism.

The applications of reductionism and the overall feeling of confidence that scientific explanations can account for the whole of nature have become essential features of scientific practice. As the next chapter will demonstrate, this inevitably has come to include human nature as well, giving rise to a conflict between scientific knowledge and other ways that traditionally have distinguished us from the rest of nature.

⌒

Items for Reflection

- Modern medical practice involves a reductionist approach whereby a specialist concentrates on a specific part of the body. However, all medications are accompanied by side effects. How does modern medication pose a challenge to a reductionist approach to treating the body?
- Is a holistic medical approach—in which the person is treated as though several bodily functions, including psychological features such as a sense of well-being, may contribute to a successful treatment—less successful because it isn't reductionist?

For Further Reading

Bacon, F. New Organon. In Works, trans. J. Spedding, R. Ellis, and D. Heath. New ed. 15 vols. New York: Hurd & Houghton, 1870–72.

Boyer, C. B. The Concepts of the Calculus. New York: Columbia University Press, 1939.

———. "The Invention of Analytic Geometry." Scientific American 180, no. 1 (1939): 40–59.

Hempel, C. G. Aspects of Scientific Explanation, and Other Essays in the Philosophy of Science. New York: Free Press, 1965.

Hoffding, H. A History of Modern Philosophy, trans. from the German edition by B. Meyer, London: Macmillan, 1900.

CHAPTER SEVEN

~

Internalizing Naturalistic Explanations

Benefit or Threat?

Despite the concluding tone of the preceding chapter, the cautiousness advocated concerning questions that science may or may not be able to answer is offered as a philosophically viable attitude only. In practice, any methodological disposition must heed the overwhelming evidence that scientific knowledge has been decisive in the material benefits humanity has come to enjoy. Of course, many environmentally related issues such as the depletion of various natural and nonrenewable resources, not to mention the availability of thermonuclear weapons that offer for the first time a level of destruction unparalleled in history, could make many of us pause as we contemplate what science has done *to* as well as *for* humanity.

The idea of progress has been closely entwined with scientific advances and given human ingenuity and cleverness. Therefore, it is perfectly reasonable to envision solutions to our most pressing problems, since many of these are the result of human activities. The field of medicine represents one of those where the benefits clearly appear to outweigh the detrimental aspects associated with the treatment of human beings as predominantly numbers in the larger context of epidemiological studies and the increasingly mechanized environment of treatment and healing practices. Who would be willing to give up the benefits of modern medicine and go back to a period of history when the average human lifespan was about thirty years?

Medical advances are a direct result of the improvement in understanding the human body as basically a machine composed of parts that break down and need to be maintained. In the United States, preventive measures are not typically associated with the medical profession, particularly since its association with pharmaceutical companies clearly places treatment ahead of prevention, as it seems more profitable. As a recent newspaper editorial amusingly stated, this dichotomy in medical practice leaves segments of the population belonging to a certain age group in the situation of being more likely to receive Viagra than a flu vaccine.

Human anatomy and physiology are just two of the fields that continue to benefit from the incredible discoveries in the life sciences. The physical sciences had traditionally led the way in the growth of knowledge about nature, beginning with Galileo's astronomical discoveries. The understanding of nature that began with the remotest areas of the universe has progressively brought us closer to our inner natures. The findings about the Earth's origins in geology, and about human origins in biology and paleontology, during the nineteenth century did not immediately translate into practical benefits for humankind in terms of technological applications. The electronic "revolution" of the early twentieth century based on the discovery of electromagnetic transmissions and the transistor, leading to the laser and the computer, to cite just two innovations, has given way to the molecular biology revolution during the latter part of the century.

These advances have been accompanied by larger societal implications, not only in terms of the technological applications and their repercussions but also in terms of the impact of the findings in these fields on the spiritual dimension of humankind. The dramatic discoveries made by Galileo about the structure of the heavens are said to have displaced humanity from its favored central position in the Creation account. The Darwinian realization is said to have further eroded the belief in the special place that humanity has traditionally enjoyed in nature.

Interestingly, the cosmological significance of being displaced from the center appears to have had a much milder impact on our view of the purpose of human existence, on the ultimate nature of the concept of the soul, and on the role of consciousness, among other things. This is perhaps due to the fact that, despite continuous advances in astronomy and in the cosmological explanations for the origin of the universe, there appears to be enough room for many of our most cherished beliefs to persist in light of the perceived lack of finality that these scientific explanations seem to have.

This is clearly not the case with the implications of the account of human origins proposed by Charles Darwin (1809–1882). Despite the fact that geological evidence and explanations point to a much older origin for the Earth than the biblical account, the fact that the continents may have looked very different in the distant past than they do today does not seem to generate the type of reaction from the general public that being told that one is essentially no different from a chimpanzee does.[1]

It is imperative to note that the metaphysical implications of the cosmological and biological origin accounts in the scientific explanations are basically identical. In both cases, the interpretation of empirical evidence in light of the theories compels scientists to make assertions about the universe and about human nature that, while being solidly grounded in scientific data, are nevertheless perceived by many nonscientists as exceeding the reasonableness of that evidence. A prominent aspect of the difference between the geological and biological explanations is the progressive nature of the mechanism that purports to account for the empirical evidence in biological evolution, natural selection, as compared to that in geological evolution.[2] The explanatory mechanism for plate tectonics that accounts for the shapes and positions of the present continents—the theory of continental drift—doesn't seem to have the teleological connotations that the concept of "fitness" as the mechanism of natural selection does. There clearly seems to be a perceived purpose to natural selection that is largely absent from geological processes.

Teleology, the view of certain processes as being directed toward a definite end or as being purpose driven, has been a feature afflicting explanations of the behavior of organisms as simple as worms since the Greeks differentiated between causality in physical processes and in biological contexts. In fact, the situation is more complicated when dealing with human beings, since ordinary events can be described as appearing to have *causes*, but human behavior definitely has *reasons*.

In a pedagogical context, the lack of teleological features in a physical process can be shown by a popular experiment that has been given to students in the Third/Trends International Mathematics and Science Study (TIMSS). They are asked to determine the effect of water temperature on the rate of dissolving of an Alka-Seltzer tablet. The experimental setup consists of a controlled environment where other variables such as the amount of water, the shape of the container, atmospheric pressure, and so forth, are kept constant. In this case, every attempt is made to isolate the situation so that the determining or independent variable is the temperature of the water. This is clearly a matter of choice, since one could argue that other variables could be used, such as the amount of energy required to bring the water to that particular temperature value depending on the means used to heat the water. Nevertheless, once the independent variable has been identified, the relationship between it and the dependent one—its effect on the rate of dissolving of the tablet, in this instance—can be investigated.

This is typical of most physical science experimentation, where causal explanations are easier to establish once the variables have been reduced to those considered independent and dependent. This is not as easily accomplished when looking at more complex systems such as organisms, where the variables that could determine the organism's subsequent behavior or actions taken can indeed be many. Of course, causality can also be very difficult to establish in physical systems that behave in a random way. Randomness can be due to complexity, chaos, or quantum uncertainty in determining the state of subatomic particles, although indeterminacy such as the latter type is not strictly the same as randomness, where all events are possible.

In biological processes, the teleological aspects of the behavior of organisms that Aristotle identified as depending on either natural (from within) or artificial (from outside) purposes have their modern counterparts in the concepts of teleomatic and teleonomic behavior as proposed by Ernst Mayr. In this structure, *teleomatic* behavior is due to external forces or conditions that regulate the goal or the end; *teleonomic* behavior is that due to an internal program or "code" of information.[3]

Teleological and anthropomorphic views about natural phenomena held by students are generally regarded as misconceptions, since the assumption is that they are attributing humanlike traits to phenomena that are not supposed to possess them. However, it is ironic that while these traits are deemed misconceptions or incorrect views when held by students, professional biologists as pointed out by Mayr cannot do their job without invoking explanations that aren't strictly "neutral," without function and value. To describe an ant colony without using the terms "queen," "soldier," "worker," and "slave" is to provide very little explanation of the respective functions the insects display. In fact, not only are these explanations loaded with value, but even observations cannot be said to be completely neutral; what the observer sees is affected by past experiences.[4]

This can be seen as part of the essential dilemma in biological explanations, including, of course, those ideas used in evolution: To attempt to explain nature using scientific statements and propositions that are supposed to be objective or value-free, and then to draw extreme conclusions that imply a function or a quality such as with the concept of fitness in natural selection, which clearly involves a value, is to engage in a form of scientism. It appears that in order to have illustrative power, biological explanations must necessarily involve anthropomorphic and teleological propositions that necessarily add an air of subjectivity to descriptions of natural phenomena. This seems inevitable, since statements made in evolutionary biology that don't have progressive connotations about how species change over time will be very limited in their scope and in their value as scientific explanations.

Curiously, the sociological implications of evolutionary theory that seem so problematic to many, given what it suggests for human beings, cease to be so striking when its origins are properly understood. The idea of natural selection didn't come to Darwin as a result of strict empirical observations either in the field or in the laboratory. There is evidence that he was trying to formulate a mechanism to account for the observed variability in species when he came across the writings of Thomas Malthus (1766–1834).[5] Malthus's ideas about the difference in birth rates by gender had, among other things, led him to conclude that the growth of populations and the availability of resources (like food) implied that nature provides mechanisms for balancing excessive growth. This concept proved to be decisive for Darwin in his search for the mechanism that became natural selection through which nature operates, since it didn't seem to call for divine intervention. It should not be surprising therefore that there are sociological implications to evolutionary theory, because the idea of natural selection *emerged* from a sociological context. Nor should it come as a surprise that the controversies surrounding evolutionary theory in terms of its implications for humanity and for life in general will likely continue unabated.

Despite the success of Darwinian evolution in accounting for the diversity of life, controversy has remained over issues like the transmission of traits such as fitness and the role of altruistic behavior, where some members of a species will sacrifice themselves to preserve the larger group, which incidentally puzzled Darwin a great deal. However, following the discovery of DNA, molecular biology has been enormously successful in accounting for altruistic behavior in terms of the transmission of genes as its explanation, and many other phenomena have been described through the quantitative understanding of genetics. It is important to mention that it was due to the crystallographic analysis, made possible with the use of x-rays, that genetics has acquired its quantitative explanatory character, with many applications in fields such as human health and agriculture, to name two.

The use of genetic information inevitably has had an impact on larger societal issues. It has also emboldened some of its practitioners to venture into areas of knowledge where their scientific credentials have enabled them to become prominent public figures. Interestingly enough, the general population does not seem to realize that in these areas of knowledge, scientific credentials can be demonstrated to be dubious sources of authority.

In addition, the main ideas in modern biology—the cell theory of life, the germ theory of disease, and the gene theory of inheritance—are all very successful because they are examples of reductionism. However, as we have already noted, reductionism needs to be understood as a methodology where our understanding must remain incomplete when we have not reached the most basic elements or constituents of our theories. Furthermore, the description of living systems solely in terms of the behavior of a cell, a germ, or a gene has been found wanting in accounting for the emergent properties and complex functions of these systems.[6]

There is a deeper level at which current understanding of biological phenomena in terms of chemical interactions is afflicted by a gap in the effort to pursue reductionism as one goes from one level to a lower one in pursuit of its logically smaller parts. Biological order expressed in terms of the order of the cell, regarded as a "super molecule" that exhibits its complex behavior at this level, has no transition to a chemical description in terms of a collection of many molecules.[7] The lack of a reverse transition from a chemical description and account to a biological one can be seen to go back all the way to the origin of life, since the basic problem of biogenesis appears to be the inability to discover a path that leads from nonlife to life.

There are cases where many scientific claims about the significance of explanations of the natural sciences for other areas of human knowledge, such as those in sociobiology (where even religion itself is claimed to have arisen through natural selection) are clear attempts to establish the authority of science in every field of human inquiry.[8] Furthermore, there are other more insidious attempts to go beyond the reduction of every feature of human beings to being a result of natural selection. The goal in some cases appears to be the creation of a social order where any source of knowledge other than science is to be excluded. To some observers, these attempts demonstrate that science appears to be positioning for a struggle against traditional views of seeing the world by expounding a totally materialistic view of life.[9] This charge is not exaggerated when one encounters an explicit admission of a commitment to materialism where a scientist can claim:

> It is not that the methods and institutions of science somehow compel us to accept a material explanation of the phenomenal world, but, on the contrary, that we are forced by our *a priori* adherence to material causes to create an apparatus of investigation and a set of concepts that produce material explanations, no matter how counter-intuitive, no matter how mystifying to the uninitiated. Moreover, that materialism is absolute, for we cannot allow a Divine Foot in the door.[10]

This statement shows that the assumption of materialism is not mandated by the scientific methodology—it is a philosophical position. Suppose that the commitment in fact was mandated by the methodology; then one could see that, based on our definition of what constitutes a scientific statement, this one fails to meet the criteria. Therefore one can legitimately ask: What can possibly justify such hostility to views of life that are not based on materialistic explanations of the nature of human beings?

Examples such as this serve to illustrate the mistrust that exists among some members of the scientific community about other views of nature that are not in conformity with what they feel science has demonstrated about natural phenomena. Consider the following statement made more recently, which confirms the commitment to naturalistic/materialistic explanations in science:

> Scientists do indeed rely on materialistic explanations of nature, but it is important to understand that *this is not an a priori* philosophical commitment. It is, rather, the best research strategy that has evolved from our long-standing experience with nature. There was a time when God was a part of science. Newton thought that his research on physics helped clarify God's celestial plan. So did Linnaeus, the Swedish botanist who devised our current scheme for organizing species. But over centuries of research we have learned that the idea "God did it" has never advanced our understanding of nature an iota, and that is why we abandoned it.[11]

We should notice the use of "a priori," where in this case there is a direct contradiction with the previous quotation. Indeed, there is agreement between the two authors concerning the need for naturalistic explanations in science. However, it is in their philosophical commitment to it that the quoted individuals completely disagree. How are we to determine who is correct—the one at the more prestigious institution?

It is important to be aware of the context in which assertions are made about the nature of human beings, the perceived lack of purpose of cosmic evolution, and the meaning of life, based on assumed scientific authority. As scientific statements, they are supposed to be based on objective, value-free conclusions. These conclusions then become the premises for the arguments

---

What is your understanding of someone's position being *methodologically* materialistic, but not *philosophically* so?

offered. However, how can one assert and defend anything that conveys a judgment of value from value-free premises?

If, on the other hand, the assertions are made as statements other than scientific, then they can be confirmed or refuted by equivalent statements that rely on the same authority as those they intend to refute, and this authority can't, of course, be science. This is where the general misconception that exists about the perceived authority with which experts in scientific fields speak on other issues can be found. The public seems to regard statements about any issues where scientific evidence is brought to bear as decisive in determining their acceptance, as when medical and legal testimony is conveyed as scientific arguments.

How prepared is a nonexpert to challenge an expert, even when the expert is speaking about an area beyond the individual's level of expertise? Given the current general perception of the authority of scientific pronouncements in every field of knowledge, not a great deal. However, as anyone who attends large scientific conferences can attest, there is a considerable deference paid to individuals from a specialized field by those from other fields, based on their own levels of expertise. Therefore, it follows that expertise ought to be more objectively exercised and recognized in general. Given the incredibly fast pace of the growth in human knowledge, no one can possibly be expected to attain the sufficient expertise to speak with unchallenged authority on more than a single (or a very limited) number of disciplines.

Why is it therefore so difficult for the public to exercise appropriate judgment when analyzing scientific claims about areas where clearly the authority of the individual who makes the claim or the claim itself has exceeded its proper logical and legitimate place and function in the discourse?

This is where scientific literacy among the general population is really needed; not so much in understanding the quantitative or technical details of whatever claims one comes across, but on being able to recognize their *legitimacy as claims*, and their function in a properly defined context. If we could convey this message as part of the products of our educational system, we would alleviate many of the conflicts in society between traditional views of life and the modern scientific version of our place in the universe. The argument here closely resembles (albeit in a different context) that offered by literary critic Terry Eagleton in his analysis of what he calls the "social devastation" brought about by economic liberalism on traditional views of life, in a theological and political context.[12]

The seemingly preeminent role of science in attempts to provide comprehensive explanatory accounts of the nature of reality can be contrasted to the role traditionally played by religious views. While one may think that ultimately all religions attempt to explain the universe and our place in it by using a transcendent Being as the ultimate source, the plethora of religious views that have and that continue to emerge appears to cast doubt on the universality of our perception of such a Being. Science, by contrast, relies on its universal character to achieve legitimate explanatory effectiveness and epistemic authority, at least as acknowledged by its practitioners. Nevertheless, since most of the human population doesn't actually understand science, it becomes very difficult to emphasize its universal character, which contains metaphysical traits. Furthermore, when these are blatantly ignored, the results are the many examples of scientism, as a clear manifestation of an unrealistic overconfidence in scientific accounts of everything.[13]

This chapter has illustrated that—just as the use of logic during the scholastic period began as a means to strengthen sacred scripture, but could also be used to undermine it—the use of scientific knowledge to account for human nature can lead to a similar undermining of traditional views of our place in the scheme of things. Scientific knowledge can be misused, for example, when pronouncements are made, based on scientific knowledge, that aren't themselves scientific. Examples have been given of instances of scientism and how to properly assess claims made in the name of science that may actually be a misappropriation of its epistemic authority.

Concepts such as fitness have levels of interpretation that range from the fundamental scientific one based on mechanistic ideas, such as the environment and organisms exhibiting variations and the result being best fits in adaptation, to misinterpretations about fitness that are clearly teleological and not based on probabilities. This shows why discussions of "objective" methods of science must be emphasized repeatedly.

⌒

Items for Reflection

- If life were to be discovered beyond Earth, how do you think this would affect our understanding of biological evolution?
- Since the current view of the observable universe is that the evidence points to a past event where its contents came into existence, can we extend the concept of evolution to astronomical considerations?

For Further Reading

Hull, D. *The Metaphysics of Evolution*. Albany: State University of New York Press, 1989.

———. *Philosophy of Biological Science*. Englewood Cliffs, NJ: Prentice-Hall, 1974.

Malthus, T. "An Essay on the Principle of Population: or, A View of Its Past and Present Effects on Human Happiness: With an Inquiry into Our Prospects Respecting the Future Removal or Mitigation of the Evils Which It Occasions." Version published in 1803, with the variora of 1806, 1807, 1817, and 1826, ed. P. James. Cambridge: Cambridge University Press, 1989.

Mayr, E. "Typological versus Population Thinking." In *Evolution and the Diversity of Life*, 26–29. Cambridge, MA: Harvard University Press, 1975.

Wade, N. *The Faith Instinct: How Religion Evolved and Why It Endures*. New York: Penguin Press, 2009.

CHAPTER EIGHT

⌐

Dispensing with Philosophy and Entertaining Limits to Human Knowledge

The preceding chapter demonstrated how the use of scientific knowledge obtained in the life sciences, when applied to other areas of human knowledge and experience, can lead to incompatible views between a humanistic or subjective character, which is the essence of artistic creativity and the contemplation of our place in the universe and relationship to the rest of nature, and the empirical evidence used to attribute these features to blind forces. If reductionism is one of the hallmarks of scientific explanation, then the issue of complex properties that emerge from simple physical phenomena but that seem irreducible to them, even without invoking supernatural explanations, remains a formidable challenge to reductionism when dealing with life processes.

The ability to understand nature through quantitative and analytical methods, which has served science so well for the last three hundred or so years, appears to be very difficult to apply to understand and predict human behavior to the same degree that we can manipulate the rest of nature. Clearly, the success in understanding the universe that began with Galileo's and Newton's discoveries about astronomical and physical phenomena should be expected to yield comparable understanding about our inner universe, brain states, and a host of mental activities. Yet despite considerable advances in physiological understanding, the depth of psychological explanations can hardly be said to have advanced to the same extent.

Of course, the implicit assumption from a scientific perspective is that it is only a matter of time until we get to the bottom of these phenomena; after all, more often than not, claims about the incompleteness in understanding nature resulting from the inability to explain certain phenomena scientifically have been shown to be premature declarations of the limits to what science can accomplish. However, as demonstrated in the discussion of the limits to reductionism in getting us to the fundamental constituents of matter and perhaps to the ultimate causes of all phenomena, it is worth considering other aspects of scientific practice that bear on the claim that science can discover the true structure of reality.

As with mental phenomena, an understanding of the processes and mechanisms that account for physical phenomena is enhanced by the use of models. Their use has become part of mainstream scientific thinking since the Newtonian account of gravitational phenomena was provided. With the advances made in understanding the microscopic and subatomic properties of matter that exceed the range of sensory experience, and in describing celestial phenomena with concepts that stretch the imagination, the use of models has become even more prevalent.

For a model to be effective, it must be *open* and allow for input, since adjustments may be needed due to mathematical expediency or upon empirical demonstrations of its predictions. However, the need for *verification*, where a model's truth is demonstrated; *validation*, where a model's arguments and methods are subjected to logical analysis; and *confirmation*, where a model's empirical support is determined, place severe methodological requirements on their use. The verification and validation of numerical models of natural systems, strictly speaking, has been found to be impossible because these are never *closed*, and this precludes their logical necessity.[1] In addition, confirmation, which often results when validity and verification are attempted, becomes impossible as well without having direct access to natural phenomena; if direct access were possible, why would we need models?

The three criteria used to distinguish scientific knowledge from other forms of knowledge—naturalistic explanations, simplicity, and testability—can now be seen to include philosophical components and metaphysically based methodological features. The first two criteria are clearly not demanded by the empirical evidence and therefore are not exclusively scientific,

---

Compare the model used in astronomy for the solar system with that used in chemistry for the structure of the atom. In what sense are they similar, and how are they different?

having emerged from the long tradition of deductive reasoning in natural philosophical inquiry that began with the Greeks and was refined during the scholastic period. The third criterion, on the other hand, depends on the inductive nature of scientific investigation, which, as we said earlier, clearly distinguishes science from other forms of knowledge. It, too, is a product of the scholastic period, but has yielded enormous dividends in understanding nature since the seventeenth century.

Therefore, we can see that the deductive nature of scientific knowledge—the aspect based on strictly logical reasoning that has effectively rendered all natural phenomena explainable in quantitative terms—is seriously undermined according to the preceding discussion. In fact, the establishment of validity and veracity that open systems fail to accomplish has also been demonstrated to afflict closed systems described by purely mathematical models, as enunciated by Kurt Gödel (1906–1978) in his Incompleteness Theorem.[2]

As far as the inductive aspects of scientific knowledge—those where causal explanations of natural phenomena are formulated—they, too, have been found to lack a logical basis given David Hume's devastating criticism of induction, as well as the practice of affirming the consequent in determining the relationship between hypotheses and experimental evidence. As an example of such practice, consider the universal use in scientific explanations of two of the most basic rules of inference in logical arguments: *modus ponens* and *modus tollens*. The first one, modus ponens, states:

- If p then q,
- p,
- therefore q.

or, symbolically:

$$p \rightarrow q, p, \therefore q \tag{I}$$

Modus tollens states:

- If p then q,
- ~q,
- therefore ~p.

with the symbolic equivalent:

$$p \rightarrow q, \sim q, \therefore \sim p \tag{II}$$

In words, the conditional part, or the direction of the implication, of both (I) and (II) states that if a premise or statement p is true, then a conclusion q follows. That is, if the antecedent is true, the consequent is also true. Modus ponens postulates that p *is* in fact the case; therefore q logically follows. Modus tollens, by contrast, postulates that it is *not* the case that q happens, or in other words, q is false; therefore it logically follows that p doesn't happen either.

If we were to replace p with hypothesis H, and q with experimental evidence EE, then the conditional part of both arguments (I) and (II) would read: "If a hypothesis (H) is true, then experimental evidence (EE) follows." The logical direction is, then, that if the antecedent is true, the consequent follows. However, in scientific explanations, the criterion of testability imposes the requirement that experimental evidence must be provided *before* a given hypothesis can be considered true. Therefore, by modus ponens (I), it would seem that the consequent (EE) would have to be established before the antecedent (H) can be accepted, and by modus tollens (II), the lack of EE would negate H. These instances are examples of affirming and denying the consequent before the antecedent can be established, which violates the logical direction of the initial statements (the conditional part of both arguments).

The truth of propositions or premises can be established only if they are logically necessary as part of closed systems, where one would have to say "if and only if" as in mathematical statements. Every other type of proposition, including scientific ones, is necessarily open unless one can absolutely control every potential circumstance that might interfere with the conclusion following from the premises. Suppose I were to tell a student, "If the weather is fine tomorrow, I will be in my office rearranging the furniture," and the next day the student finds me in the office rearranging the furniture despite lousy weather. Using (I), we would not expect to conclude that, because I am in my office, the weather must be fine. There could be many reasons why I am in the office, and some or most of them would have very little to do with the weather, although it is a factor. This example illustrates the fact that statements that allow for the possibility of extenuating circumstances render logical necessity unattainable between any predictions and the outcomes.

The implications of this conclusion for scientific knowledge are part of the extensive literature on the role of *ceteris paribus* ("everything else being the same") explanations in nature.[3] As pointed out before, the necessity of theories that eventually become causal laws is not absolute, therefore, whether we consider what we take to be the laws of nature as having been either discovered or created by us, it should be clear that claims made about the universe on their behalf cannot be determined to be true or false by the rules of logic—it must be done by experience. In this sense, we can see that the use of modus tollens (II) led Karl Popper to his classic formulation of the falsifiability principle, where scientific theories cannot be confirmed as true but can be shown to be false.[4]

The inductive character of scientifically obtained knowledge precludes the certainty that only deductive reasoning can provide, because the rules of logic cannot be invoked to decide its truth. While the use of logic in Popper's criterion of falsifiability through its use of modus tollens is clear, it is employed as a reduction to induction. In other words, the conclusion that a theory is not to be accepted if observational evidence is consistently found contrary to its predictions is forced by experience, as Hume discovered, not by logic. Therefore, we can see that the epistemic authority enjoyed by scientific knowledge, on account of its rigorous reliance on empirical criteria for verification and confirmation, is also its source of uncertainty as a form of knowledge. Prominent philosophers of science have come to regard scientific knowledge as not striving toward truth, but as seeking increasingly accurate descriptions of natural phenomena.[5]

Nevertheless, the obvious reliance on quantitative formulations of scientific explanations that has driven theoretical research from Galileo and Newton to the discovery of DNA is due to the conviction that the "language of nature" is mathematics. Consequently, one could assert that, since logic is the basis of mathematics, surely there must be a logical component to scientific investigation to be found in its theoretical foundations, despite the fact that experimental results compel us to accept or reject scientific claims largely unaided by logic.

While mathematical formulations of natural phenomena that are considered pure research, such as theoretical particle physics or cosmology, compel practitioners to regard their truth as only a function of their internal consistency, without experimental results they are likely to remain elegant mathematical formalisms, not physical descriptions. A case in point is string theory, which, despite its potential promise in linking microscopic or quantum mechanical phenomena to macroscopic or gravitational phenomena, is still regarded as a mathematical idea, not a physical theory, due to the current inability to experimentally confirm its predictions.

We can see the crucial link between the criterion of truth, expressed in the mathematical elegance of a scientific theory, and the experimentally necessary features that make science useful and that give it its distinct character as a form of knowledge. This link ought to be emphasized when the application of scientific ideas is highlighted for students, so they can understand the limitations of such ideas and appreciate their explanatory power.

Consider a demonstration of the relationship between the mathematical description of natural phenomena and the experimental determination of the theoretical predictions. Let's use the motion of a simple pendulum, a mass attached at the end of a weightless string that swings in a plane under the influence of gravity. One of the most familiar properties of the pendulum is its *period*, the time it takes to complete a whole oscillation or trip from the point of release. A typical experiment engages the student in determining the role of different variables—the length of the string, the amplitude of the oscillation (the amount that the pendulum is displaced before it is let go), the mass attached at the end of the string—on the period.

An experimental setup to demonstrate the relationship between the mathematical (theoretical) prediction of the value of the period for a given length and the actual measured period is shown in figure 8.1. The relationship determined by Galileo—that regardless of the amount displaced and the mass attached at the end, a simple pendulum's period depends only on the length of the string—can be tested with a pendulum of given length that is displaced the same amount in every trial and its period determined.

Table 8.1 shows the results of thirty trials where the pendulum was released from the same point and its period was measured.

The experimentally determined period T_{exp} from table 8.1 is

$$T_{exp} = 1.618017 \pm .000254 \text{ sec},$$

where the precision is the average uncertainty, which in this case is .000254 sec (the sum of uncertainty values divided by 30 = .000254 sec).

The theoretical period T_{th} (that predicted by the equation describing simple harmonic motion of a pendulum) is given by

$$T_{th.} = 2\pi \sqrt{\frac{l}{g}}$$

where $g = 980.3$ cm/sec^2 is the local gravitational acceleration produced by the pull of the Earth's mass on the mass at the end of the string, and $l =$ length of the pendulum. Substituting values for the variables and π, with a pendulum of length 64.5 cm, we get:

$$T_{th.} = 2(3.1416) \sqrt{\frac{64.5\text{cm}}{980.3\dfrac{\text{cm}}{\text{sec}^2}}} = 1.611736 \text{ sec}$$

Figure 8.1. Experimental setup, consisting of a pendulum of given length where its period is determined by using a photo-gate accurate to a microsecond (a millionth of a second). A protractor is attached to the support so that the angle can be measured and thus the same displacement of the pendulum is measured in every trial.

A look at table 8.1 shows that if we restrict the value of the period to the second decimal place, a hundredth of a second, then the two periods—the theoretical and the experimental—are identical. This would be the result if we were doing the experiment and the timing device could read only to the hundredth of a second. We would therefore conclude that the experimental determination of the period is exactly the value predicted by the equation,

Table 8.1. Period Analysis

Trial	Period (sec)	Uncertainty |Period – Average|
1	1.616788	.001229
2	1.617800	.000217
3	1.618300	.000283
4	1.618393	.000376
5	1.617639	.000378
6	1.618000	.000017
7	1.617900	.000117
8	1.618032	.000015
9	1.618366	.000349
10	1.618200	.000183
11	1.618000	.000017
12	1.618007	.000010
13	1.617806	.000211
14	1.617980	.000037
15	1.617300	.000717
16	1.617898	.000119
17	1.618016	.000001
18	1.617912	.000105
19	1.618299	.000282
20	1.618080	.000063
21	1.617730	.000287
22	1.618302	.000285
23	1.617796	.000221
24	1.618399	.000382
25	1.618442	.000425
26	1.618500	.000483
27	1.618081	.000064
28	1.618175	.000158
29	1.617890	.000127
30	1.618492	.000475
Average	*1.618017*	*.000254*

and the experimental error would be zero, since no difference between the values is found. Furthermore, the table shows that for the thirty trials the experimental value is the same, which bodes very well for the repeatability of the experiment.

When the value of the period is extended beyond the hundredth of a second, however, the results are very different. The full implication of the extension of the accuracy to a millionth of a second is that repeatability occurs only once—between the sixth and the eleventh trials; 93.3 percent of the time, the trials yielded a different value of the period. A graphical display of the results in figure 8.2 shows more clearly the different outcomes of attempting to measure the period of a simple pendulum when the timing mechanism is accurate to a hundredth of a second and to a thousandth of a second.

The constant value of the period is apparent from the top graph, despite the slight variation revealed by the points due to the software's statistical analysis based on the table's results. The bottom graph, on the other hand,

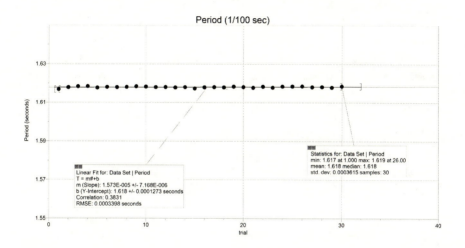

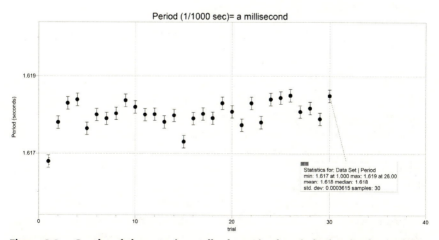

Figure 8.2. Graphs of the experimentally determined period of a simple pendulum of length 64.5 cm. The top graph shows the relationship between the period and the number of trials, where it is pretty much constant at the range of 1/100th of a second. The bottom graph shows that when the scale is at 1/1000th of a second, the period is no longer constant.

shows that there is considerable variation between 1.617 and 1.619 seconds, and using an error bar allowing for a deviation of plus or minus a hundredth of the plotted period value, only fourteen, or fewer than half, of the points lie along the straight line that represents a constant value of 1.618 seconds.

Determining the accuracy resulting from this experiment we can see that

$$\text{Accuracy} = (\text{Average } T_{exp}) - T_{th.}$$
$$= 1.618017 \text{ sec} - 1.611736 \text{ sec} = .00628 \text{ sec.}$$

As stated above, the precision, or average uncertainty, is .000254 sec. Calculating the precision as a percentage resulting from this experiment, we get:

$$\% \text{ Precision} = [\text{Precision} / \text{Average } T_{exp}] \times 100\%$$
$$= .000254 \text{ sec} / 1.618017 \text{ sec} \times 100\%$$
$$= .01569\% \approx .016\%.$$

The accuracy as a percentage is determined as follows:

$$\% \text{ Accuracy} = |(\text{Theoretical Period} - \text{Experimental Period}) / \text{Theoretical Period}| \times 100\%$$
$$= |(T_{th} - T_{exp})/T_{th}| \times 100\%$$
$$= |(1.611736 \text{ sec} - 1.618017 \text{ sec})/1.611736 \text{ sec}| \times 100\%$$
$$= .39\%.$$

The ratio of % Accuracy to % Precision (.39%/.016%) is 24.4; in other words, the result is about 24 times more precise than accurate.

According to our prior definitions of accuracy and precision, we can see that they depend on the scale of the measurements. When the periods are obtained to the hundredth of a second, the accuracy is very high; in fact, the percentage error is zero, error being defined as the deviation of the experimental value from the theoretical one, incorporating both measures of accuracy and precision. The precision, despite our being able to measure the time to the hundredth of a second, is not as high as the accuracy. However, as the precision or exactness increases from one-hundredth to one-millionth of a second, we see that the accuracy decreases to the extent noted in the last calculation; the results indicate that this experiment is much more precise than accurate.

Since accuracy is a measure of how close the experimental value is to that predicted by the theory, and precision is a measure of how repeatable the measurements are, when we increase the sensitivity of the timing mechanism we find that the experimentally determined period is 1.618017 ± .000254 seconds. What does this mean? It means that we conclude that the period can be no longer than 1.618271 seconds, and no shorter than 1.617763 seconds. How can we be certain of this? In this case, as in all measurements, one can use the uncertainty (what follows the ± symbol) to declare with certainty that *all things being equal* the experiment would yield such a result.

Table 8.1 shows that several values exceed this range; therefore, we would categorize them as being less accurate for a number of reasons, many of which are of course due to the experimenter. We should also note that none of the table values includes the theoretical period; the measurement with the highest uncertainty is the one with the closest value to the theoretical one. It is perhaps unfortunate that many students, when conducting laboratory work, think of uncertainty as "error" in the sense of being a mistake, quite apart from its intended use. The purpose of all experimental work is to attempt to decrease the range of uncertainty that every measurement carries, no matter how precise or accurate.

Let's suppose for a moment that we could in principle minimize all potential sources of uncertainty and attempt to obtain an experimental value that would be at the millionth of a second what it appears to be at the hundredth of a second. Would this give us the theoretical or "true" value? In this case, we would be relying on the mathematical correctness of the formula

$$T = 2\pi\sqrt{\frac{l}{g}} \, .$$

However, that is not possible either, since the formula is the result of an approximation. The mathematical description of the motion of the pendulum is based on the use of Newton's laws,[6] or on more advanced formulations that will inevitably yield a description known as a "differential equation."[7] When solving this equation, an assumption is made in terms of the amplitude or amount of oscillation of the pendulum, commonly referred to as the "small angle approximation." Therefore, if the formula itself is the result of an approximation, how could we ever expect to get a value of the period that is *not* an approximation?

At this point, we can see an example of the type of incremental knowledge that can be obtained when the experimental conditions are enhanced so that both the accuracy and the precision of a measurement increase. Appendix B lists a similar experimental result, but there we make sure that we approximate experimentally what has been done theoretically. In other words, since the formula

$$T = 2\pi\sqrt{\frac{l}{g}}$$

is the result of the condition that the amplitude of the oscillations be small, we decrease the angle or the amount that the pendulum is displaced in every trial to about a quarter of the value that it had when the experiment was first performed. The data in appendix B show that this time the result is about three times more precise than accurate—an enormous increase in the ability to determine experimentally the value predicted by the formula. We can see that one of the values in the table, 1.617901 seconds, comes within .003 percent of the theoretical period of 1.617848 seconds, a result rarely accomplished in the most typical experiments done by college students.

Indeed, we can approximate indefinitely the degree of agreement between theoretical and experimental results when the instruments and experimental conditions enable us to control the many sources of uncertainty and confounding variables that naturally affect all experimental work. However, as seen in the graphs of the enhanced experimental accuracy and precision, the situation remains essentially identical to the graphs in figure 8.2. While the top graph shows a fairly constant value of the period at the hundredth of a second, the bottom graph shows that the experimental period, between 1.617 and 1.619 seconds, despite its increased agreement with the theoretical value, is still uncertain and no longer constant.

Carrying the above discussion to a scenario where the agreement could be extended to the sixth decimal place, instead of to the third as allowed in our example, shouldn't this increase our confidence in the results? In other words, if the reliability of a measurement can be continually enhanced by greater precision in our instruments, the conclusions that can be reached about its significance as a "real" property of the phenomena in question can be indefinitely optimistic. Two examples will illustrate this, one from a macroscopic perspective, the other from a microscopic one:

1. The experimental confirmation of the detection of gravitational waves predicted by Einstein's general theory of gravitation—the agreement between the measurements based on signals received from space and

the value predicted by the theory—has been reported to extend to fourteen decimal places.

2. The magnetic moment of an electron has reportedly been measured in agreement with theory to the eleventh decimal place.[8]

These examples highlight the considerable confidence in the correctness of some of the most sophisticated scientific theories we have, which, while incidentally being extremely mathematically complicated, are nevertheless instances of affirming the consequent and thus deductively invalid. Therefore, for the purposes of measurement, claims made about values of any physical quantity cannot be made until measurements allow the theoretically predicted value to be sufficiently "calibrated" to become officially accepted as the "standard" or "true" value. *Standard* is a term that is easier to justify in terms of consensus; for something to be *true*, one needs more than consensus. Are true values of any physical constant to be expected independently of any measurements? It would seem that purely theoretical predictions qualify by virtue of their mathematical properties. However, as mathematical ideas are applied to natural phenomena, their degree of truth somehow changes. A good example of this realization was offered by Albert Einstein (1879–1955), who allegedly stated that, inasmuch as the laws of mathematics are certain, they do not apply to nature, and inasmuch as they apply to nature, they are not certain.[9]

Despite the aforementioned logical limitations of scientific theories, the advances in understanding natural phenomena made possible by scientific knowledge can be found not so much in the ability to arrive at predicted values of physical *constants*, but in the quantitative nature of investigation in general. This has been possible in the physical sciences by dealing with *changing* properties through the use of variables in mathematical functions, and in the biological sciences by increasingly rendering qualitative explanations as quantitative formalisms.

This chapter has served as a continuation of the concluding tone of the previous one with the purpose of demonstrating how it is that scientific methodology has turned out to be so crucially important in providing naturalistic accounts of phenomena. However, the brief discussion of the logical basis of scientific explanations also demonstrates the tentative nature of science; in other words, scientific knowledge is by definition incomplete and subject to revision. There are significant pedagogical implications in the suggestions to introduce students to the methodological foundations of scientific knowledge and practice.

As an example, consider the usefulness in this regard of an inductive process of observation, the formulation of explanations and their testing based on evidence, and the determination of their adequacy, known as the "learning cycle."

There is an extensive literature on the instructional opportunities that the cycle provides. A particularly relevant aspect is the use of If/Then/Therefore reasoning, where students are engaged in processes similar to those praticed by scientists, such as the use of the concepts of abduction and retroduction, in addition to deduction and induction.[10]

⌢

Items for Reflection

- If scientific knowledge is regarded as seeking increasingly accurate descriptions of natural phenomena, rather than striving toward "truth," as our theories progressively become more accurate, what "standard" are they getting us closer and closer to?
- How could one know that one has finally arrived at the "correct" view of what the universe looks like?

For Further Reading

Duschl, R. A. *Restructuring Science Education: The Importance of Theories and Their Development.* New York: Teachers College Press, 1990.

Mach, E. *The Science of Mechanics.* 3rd paperback ed. LaSalle, IL: Open Court Press, 1974.

Menger, K. "On Variables in Mathematics and in Natural Science." *British Journal for Philosophy of Science* 5, no. 18 (1954): 134–42.

Nowotny, H., P. Scott, and M. Gibbons. *Rethinking Science: Knowledge and the Public in an Age of Uncertainty.* Cambridge, England: Polity Press, 2001.

Smolin, L. *The Trouble with Physics: The Rise of String Theory, The Fall of a Science, and What Comes Next.* Boston: Houghton Mifflin, 2006.

CHAPTER NINE

~

Scientifically Speaking, We Know a Lot—or Do We?

Our discussion of the previous chapter led us to the conclusion that before we can claim to know anything with a level of confidence, we must have extensive confirmation and a significant degree of precision in experimentally determined measurements. However, if scientific knowledge is incomplete and anything determined experimentally must remain tentative, how can we come to know *anything* with such confidence? The attempt to acquire a perspective for an understanding of the role of science on the realm of human inquiry about nature has brought us to a point where we need to address the fact that, despite its philosophical shortcomings in providing certainty and the approximate nature of scientific knowledge, four centuries or so of immense material progress cannot be denied. What can be more evident for our study than the overwhelming influence on just about every aspect of modern life that science has acquired, rendering other forms of knowledge secondary in significance as we attempt to discover the ultimate nature of the universe?

In dealing with these forms of knowledge, empirical evidence seems to be unavailable to support views of reality that are considered, in principle, not testable such as spiritual and metaphysical beliefs. However, absence of evidence is not evidence of absence. Furthermore, how can one bring empirical evidence, or its lack thereof, to bear on issues that are declared *not* to belong to what can be studied with the tools of science? Must these issues remain extraneous to science, or is there room within scientific knowledge for their contemplation and investigation?

The rationalistic approach to studying nature that the Greeks provided and that appears to have reached a plateau in terms of what can be known quantitatively and conceptually about the universe has led no less an authority on the use of mathematical manipulation than Einstein himself to admit that the path to elemental laws is provided not by logic but by intuition.[1] This clearly allows for a link between the different forms of knowledge that we discussed in chapter 3, and it also guides inquiry that on the surface includes traits apparently considered foreign to science. On a more sophisticated level of interpretation, scientific inquiry, understood in Einstein's terms, contains a considerable amount of metaphysical speculation. However, this speculation must prepare us to take a position on the notion that what is real can be exhaustively known through science.

Einstein's claim is a result of the obvious influence of Ernst Mach (1838–1916), one of the leading figures in modern *physical thought*. To Mach, a scientific investigation of phenomena is always preceded by an instinctive, nonreflective knowledge of nature's processes. Our mental representations of the objects of sensory experience must be conceptually formulated before they can be used mathematically or otherwise. To study nature, we must begin by isolating and emphasizing what is important and by neglecting what is secondary, as Galileo taught us. Without this preconceived view of natural phenomena, methodological experimentation becomes impossible.[2]

According to our discussion of the sources of knowledge, intuition can help us in dealing with only what is knowable in the first place; if in addition we require empirical evidence through the methodology, then we must be prepared to accept degrees of certainty in our knowledge as well as limits to it. Regardless of whether we proceed inductively or deductively, and given all the demonstrated limitations of both approaches, acquiring knowledge incrementally about the universe to provide us with sufficient understanding ultimately depends on what is inherently knowable.

Students of science are often made aware of the enormous accumulation of general knowledge about nature that has been accomplished through scientific knowledge. However, the teaching seldom exposes them to the realization of how *little* is known compared to what is knowable, and even to what may be unknowable. This observation is not new of course—a similar recommendation has been made to encourage students to appreciate the strangeness of nature.[3] Nevertheless, a more concise demonstration of this kind of opportunity can be based on our current understanding of energy. I will propose a model of the amount of knowledge about the physical universe that may be possible, given what we know about electromagnetic energy. The model is based on a suggestion made by Dr. Daniel Schneck, editor of the journal *American Laboratory*.[4]

Consider the length of the electromagnetic spectrum, from the shortest known wavelengths (gamma rays) to the longest known (radio waves). Using the formula for the energy of electromagnetic components (photons),

$$E = \frac{hc}{\lambda},$$

where:

h is Planck's constant;
c is the speed of light; and
λ is the wavelength of the radiation,

one can construct a variety of lengths (not to scale, of course) from $\lambda = 0$ to $\lambda = \infty$ (that is, from the infinitesimally small to the infinitely large), as shown below.

$\lambda = 0$ **A**   (estimated)   **B** (well known) **C**   (estimated)   **D** $\lambda = \infty$

Points A, B, C, and D are meant to represent several known constants, and the following values are generally accepted for these:

A = the Planck Length ($\approx 1.6 \times 10^{-35}$ m), the shortest possible reachable distance

B = the Compton Length ($\approx 1.0 \times 10^{-12}$ m), the limit of resolution of all instruments

C = the Hubble Length ($\approx 1.3 \times 10^{26}$ m), the limit of astronomically observable distances

D = the currently expected size of the observable universe ($\approx 3.9 \times 10^{26}$ m)

The range of distance between B and C is 1.3×10^{38} m; this corresponds to the part of the universe where what is known is regarded as being highly accurate and reliable. The range of distance between A and D is 2.4×10^{61} m, which corresponds to the part of the universe where what is known is estimated. Comparing these two ranges, one can see that

$$\frac{A - D}{B - C} = 1.8 \times 10^{23},$$

or roughly speaking, the difference between A and D is 23 times greater than that between B and C. Translating this result into a pie chart, as in figure 9.2, shows that B – C represents a slice of A – D approximately equal to 5 percent of the whole pie.

5%

95%

Figure 9.2. Schematic representation of the region of the electromagnetic spectrum (given in a linear range) where what is known with a high level of confidence is only about 5 percent of the total; the much larger part, 95 percent, represents the region where what is known is estimated.

This model is decidedly optimistic, since looking at the linear representation, the regions that lie beyond D and A constitute those parts of the universe that are so currently inaccessible that we don't even know what sorts of questions to ask about phenomena that lie in such regions. Consequently, we must conclude that despite the tremendous scientific advances that have been made, what is actually known about the universe is really a tiny amount compared to what is potentially available to be investigated.

Furthermore, those regions where access to phenomena is severely limited require that we depend extensively on the use of models. As pointed out before, those models have been historically mathematical from Ptolemy to Newton. However, given the acknowledged limitations of formalisms based on logic, how else can we approach those regions of investigation? It should be emphasized that mathematical explanations continue to dominate the study of physical systems; any other areas of investigation are seen as more rigorous and therefore more credible the more they resemble the so-called hard sciences—physics, chemistry, and fields that heavily rely on methods and techniques derived from these disciplines.

It is in the study of living systems where the use of mathematics has appeared to have discrepant applications; such fields as evolutionary biology and cognitive psychology have begun to employ mathematical formalisms more recently than the physical sciences. Currently, there are divergent views about the ultimate success of mathematical explanations in appropriately describing complex biological and ecological systems, as well as emergent properties of systems that can, in principle, be simulated by simple computational techniques and models. The assumption is that even such exceedingly complex systems as living organisms, meteorological phenomena, and the functioning of the human brain can be studied and effectively described by beginning with relatively simple physical models.[5]

Two areas of evolutionary biology contain examples of varied approaches in the application of mathematical modeling to attempt explanations of complex phenomena. One displays a cautionary acknowledgment of the inherent limitations of using the concept of the rate of change to study genetic replication. The mutation rate is not a constant in the fundamental sense of those in physics, like the speed of light or Planck's constant. Rather, it is said to depend on enzyme activity.[6] The other relevant area of evolutionary biology is the use of game theory to propose a mechanism for natural selection in terms of the evolution of indirect reciprocity as it applies to individual members of a species.[7]

There are other aspects of the role of mutations in evolutionary theory that appear to yield reasonably well to statistical analysis based on randomness. However, it is interesting to note that, while the role of mutations may be best understood in terms of randomness at the level of individual variation within a population, the outcome of such variation ceases to be random at another level—that resulting from increased adaptation to a particular environment. Despite the likelihood of quantitative manipulation, the use of reductionism in molecular genetics and developmental biology constitutes a limit to what can be known about organic functions, behavioral traits and conditions, and other biological processes. This is an outcome of descriptions of systems that begin by interacting chemically and end up at the level of the organism, although they are highly speculative in their use of what is considered "strong" reductionism.[8]

The use of reductionism in general scientific accounts exhibits serious limitations due to its metaphysical character and evident traits as an example of scientism, where its practice can be more actively attributed to faith in its effectiveness than to its being logically demonstrated. This is a result of its seductively compelling appeal as an explanatory mechanism originating from the need to unify scientific accounts from the behavior of small organisms to a "theory of everything."[9] We need to remember, however, that even if an all-encompassing scientific theory were to be found that *could* unify the macroscopic and microscopic phenomena that are currently at odds, this alone would not constitute sufficient grounds for its acceptance. A theory of such magnitude would still have to be relentlessly tested and its predictive features would, in a sense, be expected to be basically infinite.

Another opportunity to highlight the incomplete and tentative nature of scientific knowledge comes from an area where it is important to demonstrate some of the features of mathematical reasoning. These can be found in disciplines where the attempts to apply mathematics have been found to be resistant to, or perhaps incompatible with, inductively based explanations, for example, the study of consciousness. Investigations of mental activity have led many researchers to conclude that given the empirical evidence, theories that are strictly based on physical assumptions seem to lack the explanatory substance required by such phenomena.[10]

The ability to simulate brain processes that include consciousness, or our awareness of our mental activity, has received a great deal of attention in the field of artificial intelligence (AI) ever since computers became a tool of investigation. Many interesting results have been obtained by simulating brain activity with computational models that assume strictly physical inputs, where the outputs are the result of these and other physical processes in the brain. Despite many adherents to the explanations of consciousness provided in the area of AI, a highly speculative and promising view represents a bold and drastic attempt to unify the two most successful, although currently mutually exclusive, physical theories: quantum mechanics and relativity.[11]

An interesting aspect of this view is that it considers mental states as being fundamentally nonalgorithmic, or essentially noncomputable.[12] This represents a break with the long-held expectation that mathematics could ultimately provide the means to explain natural phenomena. Curiously, prominent scientists have expressed their bewilderment concerning the explanatory power of mathematics in the natural sciences.[13] Other scholars are not surprised about the immensely successful ability to describe the universe that mathematics provides; for them, mathematics succeeds in the task not just because it effectively describes the universe but because the universe *is* a mathematical structure.[14] Nonetheless, to declare mathematics insufficient at this point in the scientific attempts to understand some aspects of natural phenomena is to adopt a curious perspective.

The theme of this chapter can be summarized by acknowledging that our understanding of consciousness currently represents an area where we clearly don't know a lot, despite considerable advances in investigation facilitated by technology. We should also remember that science not only has provided the means for the discovery and establishment of many disciplines where our knowledge of nature has increased dramatically but also has come to be regarded as perhaps our primary means to generate new knowledge, mostly for the common good. Still, how much of this knowledge is to be believed when the predominant way to arrive at it is through experimentation, where the conditions regarded as being "natural" really aren't?[15]

Recall that induction involves the use of conditions where phenomena are considered and manipulated under circumstances that are, in a sense, artificial. The recommendation by Popper that induction ought to be seen as a limitation of scientific knowledge, despite its proven effectiveness in conveying empirically reliable knowledge, naturally follows. The demonstration that we know very little of the universe, as evidenced by the proposed model in this chapter, can be extended to other disciplines and supported by an analysis of the role of scientific theories.

The traditional distinction mentioned in chapter 3 between correspondence and coherence as a criterion for the truth of statements about the world can be restated in terms of our understanding of what a theory is. Comparing a territory to a map is a useful metaphor for comparing the acknowledged existence of an independently real universe to our attempts to understand it.[16] The map is limited in its ability to reproduce the territory by the amount of detail that can be incorporated into it. Increasing the amount of detail may enhance reproducibility, but it may also confound the reader as to what the totality of the area looks like. Conversely, a very large scale may give an accurate description of the totality of the terrain, but it will inevitably leave out most of the details, where important information may be found.

In summary then, we see that there are several instances where the limits to what we can know about nature are due to the methodology we employ, including the use of reductionism, the empirical nature of inductive knowledge, the power of mathematics as an explanatory mechanism, and theories as our most comprehensive worldviews. Additionally, the control of variables and the use of models require techniques designed to facilitate experimental observations that must conform to predetermined questions dictated by the theoretical contexts under which they can be entertained. What other aspects besides the incompleteness and tentative nature of scientific knowledge do we need to consider in our endeavor to help students become scientifically literate? The next two chapters deal with these.

As an example of the need to obtain information about phenomena in nature, investigate the use of maps in London during the nineteenth century to solve the problem of a cholera epidemic. Concentrate on the use of the locations of water supply stations and the flow of the Thames River in your analysis. How did they solve the problem?

This chapter has been designed to dispel a common misconception among students that is largely a pedagogical consequence and that likely inhibits the inherently fascinating nature of scientific practice. Typical science instruction emphasizes factual knowledge and fails to convey to students how little is actually known about the universe. "Science" is constituted by a body of knowledge, but it is also a unique way of seeing the world that involves critical thinking. We could be more successful in promoting scientific literacy and producing more reflective citizens if we effectively convey to students how little we know about what is potentially knowable.

Items for Reflection

- Can you think of other graphical ways to represent the information discussed in the pie chart representation (figure 9.2)?
- Some people feel that emphasizing to students how little we know about the universe could actually backfire in getting them interested in scientific careers, in the sense that they would feel powerless to contribute in any significant way to an increase in knowledge. Do you agree?

For Further Reading

Kline, M. *Mathematics and the Search for Knowledge*. New York: Oxford University Press, 1985.

Maynard Smith, J. *Evolution and the Theory of Games*. Cambridge: Cambridge University Press, 1982.

O'Hear, A. *Beyond Evolution: Human Nature and the Limits of Evolutionary Explanation*. Oxford, England: Clarendon Press, 1997.

Wilson, E. O. *Sociobiology*, Cambridge, MA: Harvard University Press, 1975.

Ziman, J. *Real Science: What It Is, and What It Means*. Cambridge: Cambridge University Press, 2000.

CHAPTER TEN

~

The Need for a Context

Scientific discoveries and the advancement of knowledge do not occur in isolation—they require a context. The goal of this chapter is the provision of a context for a proper understanding of the development and role of scientific knowledge, along with the implications for other areas of inquiry. Now that we have covered considerable (although necessarily abbreviated) aspects of the historical part of the required context, it is appropriate to consider in more depth the meaning for the development of scientific literacy of the ideas discussed in the previous chapter. And there are few more instructive opportunities available to demonstrate to students various philosophical aspects of the context than the inherently fascinating conclusions drawn from our current understanding of subatomic phenomena.

As we have seen, the clearly discernible influence of a philosophical outlook on the study of nature that can be considered a precursor to our current view is that of the scholastic period, particularly during the thirteenth century.[1] The need to investigate nature in ways that led to the practice of systematic experimentation was prompted by the philosophical perspective provided by the Aristotelian worldview. Similarly, during the seventeenth century, the scientific revolution brought about by Galileo and Newton, among others, was made possible by the philosophical perspective promoted by Francis Bacon, with his thoughts on the practical aspects of knowledge obtained from a study of natural phenomena, and to some extent by the mathematical aspects of René Descartes's (1596–1650) philosophical system.[2] It is the latter's system that is more relevant for our purposes.

The use of mathematics as a tool or a language was drastically different for Descartes than it was for Newton. The former was interested in a more causally complete understanding of nature, whereas the latter was more pragmatic in his approach, relegating the need to hypothesize to a lower level than the need to model and calculate. Unlike the intellectual climate of the thirteenth century where Aristotelian philosophy had provided the dominant context, Newton and Descartes represented two competing mechanistic philosophical schools.[3] As an example, the discovery of the law of gravitation and the means by which Newton demonstrated how it worked required action at a distance without the interacting objects making contact. This exposed Newton's approach to the criticism that he was bringing occult features into the explanation, since Descartes's system required a "plenum," or continuous interaction by contact, between all objects in space.

Newton realized that a force transmitted through space without an intervening medium was methodologically unsound at the time. Nevertheless, it was through his insistence on demonstrating the correlation between quantitative theoretical predictions and experimental measurements that he accomplished an unprecedented degree of precision and accuracy in describing natural phenomena. This represents the triumph of the Newtonian view over the Cartesian one and determined the eventual path followed by scientific investigation ever since.[4] The philosophical justification for the success of science in describing and explaining natural phenomena since Newton has been its utility, represented by predictive power and testable opportunities as well as mathematical simplicity and elegance.

The intellectual climate during the nineteenth century in which the introduction of Darwinian evolution took place was also dominated by a particular philosophical perspective. Besides the sociological influence of Malthus's ideas on Darwin's views, an important factor in the introduction of natural selection as the mechanism for evolution was the reigning philosophy of science in England at the time. Darwin was very concerned that his theory fit the methodological requirements promoted by the most influential philosopher of science in the 1830s, the famous astronomer John

---

Descartes is said to be the originator of the modern dualistic view of humans in which we have a physical component, the body, but also a nonmaterial entity, the soul. Certain indigenous views of nature see the Earth as sharing a living or animate feature with humans. How are these views incompatible with the view held by Descartes?

F. W. Herschel (1792–1871).[5] To Herschel, the best example of a law was a quantitative one, and the best of those was Newton's law of universal gravitation. Of course, the philosophical aspects of evolutionary theory were not relevant only at the time of the theory's inception—they continue to be debated to this day.[6]

The changes in perspective in the scientific outlook brought about by relativity and quantum mechanics in the early part of the twentieth century have produced the most successful physical theories to date. The technological applications of these incredibly mathematically successful theories are only now beginning to become apparent. However, it is their philosophical implications that are problematic. It is significant that, given the frenetic pace of technological innovation as well as computational improvements since the invention of computers, the perplexing aspects of these theories concerning ideas of causality, space, and time remain unabated after nearly eighty years.

Despite the fascinating predictions made by relativity that have shaken the foundation of some aspects of humanity's understanding of space and time, as well as the history and scale of the observable universe, this macroscopically dominant theory is still considered classical in the sense of extending the Newtonian legacy of being deterministic. Deterministic theories contain mathematical descriptions in the form of equations whose solutions are considered "real" in the numerical sense. As an example, a solution to Newton's second law of motion stated algebraically can yield a value for either the velocity or the position of an object. This theoretical value can be experimentally compared to an actual measurement of the object's property, whether position or velocity.

Quantum mechanics, on the other hand, depends on a mathematical formalism in which the solutions to the equations are regarded as probabilistic. Consequently, the position or velocity of a subatomic particle, such as an electron, is interpreted differently from that of a macroscopic object of the type described by classical physics.[7] The measurable properties of matter at the subatomic level, then, must be understood as states of observable features that are *probabilities.*

There are two types of probabilities: objective and subjective. The first is a result of randomness or the propensity of an event to occur. The second is a measure or a statement about our ignorance of the outcome.[8] Deterministic theories are incompatible with objective probabilities, since these would limit the effectiveness of such theories to reliably predict regularly occurring phenomena, such as those found in Newtonian mechanics and the dynamics of ordinary objects.

A mainstream philosophical interpretation of quantum mechanics adopted by some of its most prominent originators has come to be known as the "Copenhagen interpretation,"[9] because it was heavily influenced by Danish physicist Niels Bohr (1885–1962). The crucial adoption of the interpretation of the features of subatomic phenomena as subjective probability is to be found in the work of Max Born (1882–1970). In the statistical interpretation of quantum theory, Born explicitly equates probabilistic statements of the physical properties of subatomic phenomena as being a result of the observer's ignorance.[10] This particular adoption has been criticized on philosophical grounds because it renders statements about the random occurrence of events, such as radioactive decay or the odds of someone winning the lottery, as a result of our ignorance of the initial conditions of these processes.[11]

Nevertheless, common interpretations of probability rely on Bayes's Theorem, or the Bayesian calculus of probability, in which subjective and objective elements appear as combined measures of a state of knowledge about statistical outcomes.[12] Specific applications of Bayesian statistics to measurements and expectation values have long been a staple of experimental physics.[13] Good examples of these applications are seriously needed in showing students how this has come about.

There are other instances in quantum mechanics where traditional distinctions in measurement and experimentation in general are blurred, such as the "collapse" of the wave function that describes the state of any subatomic particle (from a probability value to an actual quantitative result). In this case, there is no longer a distinction between the observer and what is being observed,[14] or between possibilities and actuality.[15]

The difficulties for anyone who tries to understand quantum mechanics are not just mathematical. The apparently absurd conclusions that have puzzled even the theory's originators are due to its philosophical implications. Indeed, Bohr's famous dictum "Anyone who is not shocked by quantum theory has not understood it"[16] succinctly conveys the point. Yet, even if the philosophical objections raised against the quantum interpretation of the probabilistic features of subatomic phenomena are ignored (given the tremendous success that quantum mechanics has enjoyed), a significant challenge to an understanding of the theory remains.

The current situation is similar to that in the seventeenth century between the Newtonian and Cartesian worldviews. The prominence of the Newtonian perspective is due to the success in its application of the mathematical formalism, particularly in predicting experimental results. This is a form of *instrumentalism*, an attitude that disregards attempts to understand a theory by emphasizing its explanatory success.[17] If we concede that the impressive degree of agreement between quantum theory and experimental evidence is enough to force upon us an instrumentalist attitude, based on the acknowledgment that the probabilities encountered in subatomic phenomena are the result of the observer's lack of knowledge, then we are faced with more difficulties.

Consider a situation where an object is hidden in one of three similar containers on a table. If we are asked to predict where the object actually is, we must agree that, based on probability, the likelihood that we shall find it under any of the containers is 1 in 3. If upon uncovering a chosen container we find that the object isn't there, we conclude that we were incorrect in choosing that particular one, but the initial probability remains unchanged. The probability that the object will now be under either of the remaining two containers is 1 in 2. If we now uncover one and find the object, then we succeed in our task. But the probability remains unchanged; it was 1 in 2 whether or not we opened the correct one. The object's actual presence and its probable likelihood of being there are separate.

However, if the object is a subatomic particle like an electron, then according to quantum theory we are forced to conclude that when we find the particle under the correct container, the probability that it was there and the particle *being* there are identical! In other words, half the particle was there all along,[18] and it only becomes the complete particle that is found when the observation is made. In this particular case, the existence of the particle and the act of observing it are inextricably linked.

This type of realization leads us to a conundrum in which we are required to regard subatomic phenomena as following very different rules from macroscopic, everyday objects, including their perceptual properties. The human role in experimentation has taken center stage in the determination of properties of natural phenomena, where the measuring apparatus now includes the observer.[19] There are areas of research where this feature of quantum theory has received considerable attention, particularly in studying the large-scale properties of the universe, a field known as quantum cosmology.

A particularly interesting alternative interpretation of quantum phenomena is the "many-worlds interpretation," a theory of measurement that attempts to describe the universe beginning with the role of the observer.[20] Of significance for our discussion is the fact that using this theory, some scholars are arguing on philosophical grounds for a reinterpretation of quantum mechanics. In particular, the use of Ockham's principle is a prominent feature of the reasons why it is felt that the Copenhagen interpretation is dynamically unacceptable.[21]

A discussion of the philosophical features of quantum mechanics is an excellent opportunity to engage students in considerations of the role of theories on experimentation and on the interpretation of data. As stated previously, one of the identified shortcomings of students' views of scientific knowledge is their belief that well-tested hypotheses gradually become theories. This implies a sort of one-directional flow in students' perception of the way science is performed, from the simplicity of a hypothesis (often seen as an educated guess) to the more complex status attributed to theories. They appear to lack a perspective where such flow can be seen as bidirectional or cyclic. In other words, they think of data as being used to generate hypotheses that eventually become theories, but don't readily see theories as influencing how experimentation is done, how data are interpreted, how inferences are drawn, and how hypotheses are eventually formulated. Stated somewhat differently, theories are not correctly seen as broader explanatory frameworks needed to guide hypotheses testing.[22]

There are supportive findings about science process skills from international assessments that indicate that most students

- are unable to understand complex modeling in the design of an investigation,
- cannot identify relationships between various scientific concepts in developing explanations, and
- cannot formulate arguments by a synthesis of evidence from multiple sources.[23]

These epistemological features of students' understanding of scientific knowledge must be incorporated into instructional instances with techniques such as "predict-observe-explain" (POE) where an area of modern scientific understanding of microscopic phenomena (which students find interesting and stimulating) can be used to foster their development of scientific literacy involving critical thinking skills.

The mathematical aspects that probability theory applications convey are often difficult to incorporate into instructional tasks in such a way that students can clearly see how they are relevant to advances in our understanding of the material world. Quantum phenomena discussions properly designed to engage students in discussions that do not require extensive formulaic manipulations also allow for an incorporation of the tentative nature of scientific knowledge.

In conclusion, it should be made apparent to students that progress needs to be made in the philosophical aspects of current scientific views of the structure of matter, despite the enormous mathematical and experimental improvements to these theories. The belief that the philosophically perplexing features of quantum phenomena will turn out to be nonissues, given the enormous success of the theory, is clearly a form of instrumentalism consistent with Newton's own view of gravity. In any case, we must accept that, despite our ability and cleverness in using such theories to explain nature, a gap in understanding remains and is an indication of the limits to human knowledge about the natural world.

Why is it a limit to knowledge? The mainstream Copenhagen interpretation claims that our ignorance in knowing beforehand the properties of subatomic phenomena, even with the aid of mathematics, is not just a result of our methods of investigation. The inability to predict the properties of subatomic phenomena in the same way we can predict the properties of macroscopic objects is apparently due to the inherent uncertainty in the phenomena themselves, not just our ignorance of the properties.

The philosophical implications of twentieth-century physical theories have been emphasized in this chapter to illustrate the difficulties in understanding microscopic phenomena that successful scientific theories have generated, despite the enormous improvements made over earlier attempts to understand nature, particularly at the macroscopic level. This discussion provides a basis for the consideration that there may be limits to what scientific knowledge can provide, largely due to its provisional character.

⌢

Items for Reflection

- What comes first: a theory or the facts upon which the theory is based?
- How is the Copenhagen interpretation consistent with an anthropomorphic (human-centered) perception of reality?
- How does quantum mechanics relate to constructivist views of epistemology, where the learner constructs a representation of reality, rather than acquiring it from external sources?

For Further Reading

Popper, K. R. *Conjectures and Refutations: The Growth of Scientific Knowledge.* London: Routledge, 1963.

Shapere, D. "The Concept of Observation in Science and Philosophy." *Philosophy of Science* 49, no. 4 (1982): 485–525.

Ziman, J. *Reliable Knowledge: An Exploration of the Grounds for Belief in Science.* Cambridge: Cambridge University Press, 1978.

CHAPTER ELEVEN

~

The Rightful Place of Science in Society

What are the implications for our goal, to understand the larger societal role that scientific knowledge has come to play, of the previous discussion of contemporary debates concerning the metaphysical and philosophical aspects of perhaps the most successful scientific theories?

Since the debates stem from the need to understand scientific knowledge and for communities to use it in making important decisions, it is likely that some solutions may be found by exploring the ways in which that can be facilitated. Given the complexity of the interactions between science and other fields of knowledge that exists in the modern world, a denial on the part of scientists of this imperative may alienate them from the rest of society. In fact, examples can be found of appeals to the scientific community in particular, and to the intellectual community in general, to reflect on the importance of metaphysical aspects of scientific practice.[1]

To popularize scientific explanations so that the utility and wonderful vistas offered by science about the nature of the universe can be grasped and its technological fruits properly employed, the scientific community needs to be more transparent in its dealings with the general public. This is also an area where the issue of scientific literacy looms large: Popular media depictions, the teaching of science, the dialogue between science and government, and the general perception of scientific work and discovery by the nonexpert community must all converge onto a new perspective.

Science slowly emerged from natural philosophy and acquired a distinctive methodology in the seventeenth century. It has become such a dominant and successful way to investigate nature ever since precisely because its practitioners have been willing to accept that, methodologically speaking, scientific knowledge will always be incomplete and subject to revision. The evident intrusion of scientific explanations into most other fields of human knowledge, very often resulting in scientism, has created an atmosphere of near reverence for anything that can be expressed scientifically. The expectation that science will ultimately provide the answers and solutions to all of humanity's problems may have become the prevalent disposition in some circles, but should this be a universal attitude?

The self-appropriated epistemic authority that often accompanies scientific accounts of contemporary views on issues that have puzzled the best minds in history displays a curiously dogmatic character. There is sometimes a level of intellectual intolerance for views that don't rely on empirical confirmation when offered against or alongside scientific ones.

Interestingly, the rejection of competing theories, particularly physical ones, is not done strictly on empirical grounds, since it would be virtually impossible to test every claim. Instead, they have historically been, and are still, considered scientifically false based primarily upon criteria such as a lack of simplicity and an insufficient explanatory force or predictive power.[2] Since the hallmark of scientific practice is experimental confirmation, and if scientific knowledge is provisional even if empirically validated, it is intriguing to see the adoption of a metaphysical stance—that the universe is physically comprehensible—as a nonempirical and *permanent* feature of scientific knowledge.[3] If the essence of rationality is critical thinking, this methodological approach seems ad hoc.

It is important to emphasize that scientific theories must in principle be falsifiable, and thus are likely to be rendered false in the future. However, the property of being falsified must be based on empirical grounds, not on some stance which by definition admits of no experimental dependence. A metaphysical predisposition dictates what experiments are conducted and how the data are to be interpreted. This is the essence of the concept of theories as broadly explanatory networks that needs to be communicated to students.

Additionally, the falsifiability criterion as advocated by Karl Popper's reduction to induction—the methodologically dictated need to subject the epistemic authority of science to experience, discussed previously—makes it more difficult to evaluate scientific theories at an epistemological level, where competing explanations could receive comparable attention. In other words, the theory-relative aspects of scientific explanations cannot be easily accessible to both novices and experts, if it is in the empirical arena where confirmation or refutation is to be expected. The position expressed here is that we need a perspective that incorporates ontological realism (the assumption that there is a reality that science gradually uncovers) combined with epistemological pluralism, not relativism—a progressive view that takes into consideration alternative and defensible interpretations of scientific findings.

The use of the map metaphor introduced in chapter 9 provides the justification for ontological reality, as expressed by the territory, and epistemological plurality, as expressed by the various maps designed to represent it. These maps necessarily include mathematics inasmuch as it can constitute both structure and function, fundamental aspects of scientific theories. A particularly important issue in the evaluation of competing views inherent in such epistemological plurality is the consideration of the proposed "migration" of scientific knowledge from its traditional academic setting to a postacademic one.[4] An example of such a transition is the Genome Project, which is typified by the intense competition between independent laboratories and research groups for applications of the latest discoveries in molecular biology to all sorts of other areas, in many of which serious ethical considerations are in their infancy.

The opportunities in a postacademic setting for enrichment in terms of the incorporation of formally accepted metaphysical features and other perhaps desirable traits into scientific knowledge can also be accompanied by further erosion of scientific literacy and, of course, by an increase in scientism along with its many deplorable humanistic consequences.

The pedagogical value of engaging students in inquiry-based, guided discovery activities lies in the fact that an emphasis on critical thinking skills, such as predicting the outcome of an experimental task, allows for discussions of confirmation and refutation at a developmentally critical level for the students. The value of using predictions is that they put the learner in a context of discovery, where disconfirmation can be more valuable than confirmation, as claimed by Popper's view.

An emphasis on the value of refutation represents an economy of thought, since deciding between competing views is more likely to occur when the range of possible explanations is reduced by actively seeking to adopt a skeptical rather than a confirmatory disposition in experimental interpretations.[5] If we were consistent in applying Popper's criterion that a theory can be made false by disconfirming evidence, rather than allowing the hypotheses generated by the theory to pass the empirical tests, we could actually better implement the incorporation of Ockham's principle into scientific knowledge.

Passing an empirical test is not the same as demonstrating the truth of a hypothesis. In fact, a serious criticism of scientific testing has existed since

French physicist Pierre Duhem (1861–1916) enunciated what has become known as the Duhem-Quine Problem. It basically states that no single hypothesis can be isolated from a group of hypotheses, and so experimental confirmation of one hypothesis does not automatically rule out the remaining ones.[6] This is a perennial feature of scientific investigation, and we must convey it to students as part of their engagement in the development of scientific process skills.

The comparison by Duhem of hypotheses-testing in scientific practice with medicine is very appropriate. A good lesson comes when it is made clear to students that there is no medication without side effects. A physician treats an ailment by concentrating on a specific organ, or on one of the body's systems, but it must be done without being able to completely isolate it from the rest of the body (following a considerable process of elimination), which is the reason for side effects. In scientific hypothesis-testing, refutation takes place within a similar context where competing hypotheses are rendered less likely, but not completely irrelevant. This process follows the typical application of the Bayesian logic of probabilities.

To complete the cycle that provides the context for a proper understanding of scientific knowledge and practice, it is also important to note the sociological aspects of scientific practice. These are very significant in the development of scientific literacy and can be effectively incorporated into a discussion of the larger context, provided that the epistemological rather than the empirically methodological aspects of scientific practice are highlighted. The methodological aspects of scientific practice have been adopted and emulated in sociology in attempts to make the discipline more quantitative and perhaps predictive.[7] Ironically, the potentially humanistic aspects of scientific knowledge are thus undermined by attempting to render sociology more scientific, despite the invaluable insights and contributions of sociological perspectives on scientific methodology.

In order to make science and scientific literacy more appealing to students, the various cultural and societal aspects that influence scientific practice need to be made much more visible and tangible during instruction. An analysis of case studies, such as those that involve laboratory practice at research institutions comprised of individuals from many nationalities and cultural backgrounds, can convey to students a more realistic flavor of the way science is carried out at these levels.[8] This type of analysis offers dramatic confirmation of the fact that, in empirical settings, not only is inductive knowledge being generated, but the validity of deductive knowledge is being determined more often by sociological than by logical considerations. Hence, scientific knowledge is arrived at not only through intuition, as Einstein declared, but as a result of consensus—something rarely evident to students in their early stages of preparation.

Another important consideration is the role of factors extraneous to scientific practice in the replication of experiments that test for the existence of novel phenomena, as in the case of the detection of gravitational waves. These waves were predicted by Einstein's general theory of relativity early in the twentieth century, but they have not been convincingly detected yet. An analysis of a prominent case claiming the detection of such waves illustrates that the debate that ensued following this announcement was influenced more by personality conflicts and perceptions of honesty than by the three criteria identified as being essential to determine what constitutes scientific knowledge. In other words, the naturalistic, simplicity, and testability criteria that should have been applied to this purported scientific discovery became secondary, and issues of credibility that were often based on other criteria became prominent in its apparent resolution.[9]

A persistent theme of this text has been the imperative to provide in an academic setting, as well as for the population at large, a perspective where our views about life in general can be properly aided by the enormous benefits that can be obtained through science. But how is this to be accomplished in an atmosphere of mutual suspicion, resulting from a clash where modernity has forced most individuals who adopt a scientific view of life to regard those who don't as being somehow ignorant and hindering progress, while they, in turn, are perceived as dismissive of anything that is not scientific?

This form of superficial relativism stems from a lack of perspective on the clash between traditionally religious sources of morality and behavior, and the ideas that emerged from the seventeenth and eighteenth centuries, namely, the scientific revolution and the Enlightenment.[10] It should be made clear that the perceived clash between scientific and nonscientific views of life, such as evolution and religious views on Creation, is not universally endorsed by either the scientific or religious communities. A case in point is the recent development by the American Association for the Advancement of Science of the Dialogue on Science, Ethics, and Religion.[11] This program aims to foster an atmosphere of discussion with mutual respect for both religious and scientific views, in particular Christian teachings and the theory of evolution. It stands in contrast to other intellectual movements where the aim is to provide an explanation for ethical behavior, but following strictly secular approaches.[12]

Discussions of religious beliefs may emerge from scientific investigations; however, it seems entirely appropriate for ethical and moral behavior discussion to be considered as a result of speculations based on evolutionary evidence. This situation can be contrasted to the debate between intelligent design and evolutionary explanations. In this case, despite the good intentions of some of its proponents resulting from a reaction to the perceived invasive nature of evolution as an explanation of life, we can see that the movement is nevertheless an example of scientism.

As stated at the outset, we need a new perspective on the incorporation of scientific knowledge into other areas of human endeavor. An inherent characteristic should be the acknowledgment that a scientific view on anything is a temporary one, not the final word. The failure to accept this betrays the original intent of the scientific view of nature and undermines the development of scientific literacy that is indispensable when attempting to tackle many of the issues facing us today.

So, what should a new perspective on scientific knowledge look like? We might begin with the recommendations in the *National Science Education Standards* concerning the perception among many students that scientific knowledge is infallible. Students must learn that there are things that science can and cannot do,[13] and that to develop critical skills—*to think like scientists*—students must be engaged in inquiry-based tasks where one often must approach a problem in relative ignorance.[14] The *fallibility* of science must be made apparent to students.

In a broader sense, the philosophical aspects of scientific practice should be acknowledged more prominently, particularly in areas of investigation where subjectivity is routinely ruled out as scientifically invalid. An example is the study of mental activity. Brain processes that lead to our awareness of consciousness result in individual accounts, or first-person descriptions. These experiences are systematically disregarded in favor of third-person accounts that are based on perceived behavior and are thus accepted as being objective.[15] But why should a subjective lack of knowledge on the part of the observer concerning subatomic phenomena according to quantum mechanics be more acceptable than the subjective possession of some form of knowledge about one's own mental activity? To exclude first-person accounts of mental phenomena seems unwarranted on empirically methodological grounds, thus becoming a metaphysical perspective.

How does intelligent design qualify as a contemporary example of the failure to heed St. Augustine's advice concerning statements made in the name of religion, but based on empirically obtained knowledge?

Moreover, there is a logically consistent occurrence of a collapse of the distinction at the subatomic scale between the observer and what is being observed in measurement and of the reported independence of subject and object in the act of introspection.[16] The role of consciousness in quantum mechanics has provided a need to reexamine traditional views about mental phenomena, to an extent that may challenge the metaphysical assumption that mental activity is just an emergent property of brain processes—in other words, that there is nothing besides physical activity involved in consciousness.[17] In fact, the role of consciousness has come to occupy a prominent place in the philosophy of science in general.[18]

Several philosophical features introduced by Plato and Aristotle continue to animate scientific investigation. These are the assumption of the existence of mathematical truths independent of our confirmation, the relationship between potentialities and actuality in quantum mechanics, and the inability to make statements about the future without having to invoke the principle of "all things being equal."[19] The latter feature can be clearly traced to its Aristotelian origin, and it is a crucial component in the nonexpert population's ability to distinguish between scientific predictions and scientific forecasting. It is simply false to consider scientific practice as having divorced itself from its philosophical origins altogether.

Could future scientific accounts of certain phenomena incorporate elements traditionally considered unacceptable as part of its explanations? In current cosmological theory, ideas such as dark matter and dark energy—which are in practice necessary, but in principle undetectable by existing technology—are seriously considered. Of course, while the use of such concepts seems imperative at the moment, it is hoped that there will be experimental evidence for them in the future. How different is it to assume that there is a component to mental activity, consciousness, that serves as an explanation for many introspective and contemplative features of such phenomena, even if it is currently undetectable with existing technology?

Could the incorporation of features traditionally regarded as being outside the scientific criteria listed in chapter 1, particularly the naturalistic criterion, help to provide not only scientific explanations but a richer philosophical perspective? They could, if they cease to be considered as being supernatural—that is, if the metaphysical outlook allows for a more "holistic" approach. Traditional scientific materialism can continue to be paradigmatic of the methodology, but it doesn't have to be the dominant philosophical view. It is in the latter context that science can be of most use in our ongoing quest to understand nature and our place in the universe.

The metaphysical and sociological aspects of scientific knowledge have been emphasized in this chapter as a result of the philosophical issues discussed in the previous one. The goal is to provide a larger context where science can be more readily seen as a human activity and that, based on sociological and philosophical considerations, should be more encompassing of alternative explanatory structures. A particularly desirable outcome would be to see that dogmatism is to be avoided in scientific knowledge if humanity is to continue to benefit from its use to solve our most pressing problems.

The mysterious has been readily accepted by some of the greatest scientific minds as well as the greatest philosophers. It still serves to motivate many in their awareness of certain transcendental features of perceived reality. Science as a human activity should not be expected to provide the ultimate answers since it cannot even ask all the questions. Our appreciation of the mystery of existence should be enhanced by this realization, not reduced to the speculative nature of our quest to understand.

This chapter, then, has served as the contextual setting where the historical, philosophical, and sociological features of scientific knowledge are to be integrated into a comprehensive humanistic perspective of what science is and what it *should do* for us. The next and last chapter will recapitulate the themes that we have explored, with the intent to provide such a perspective.

CHAPTER TWELVE

~

Concluding Reflections

The main objective of this book has been to demonstrate the *tentative* rather than *definitive* aspects of science. We need to resist the modern tendency to regard scientific knowledge as the only kind of authentic knowledge—that forms the basis of scientism. This inclination is particularly evident in disciplines that attempt to provide scientific approaches to and explanations of complex phenomena, such as those in the human sciences. In these instances, soft-core scientism, the belief in the primacy of science to provide guidance to human affairs, is a dubious approach.

The last two chapters dealt with the difficult but necessary discussions of the philosophical and sociological aspects that must be considered if we are to see scientific knowledge as a "human" activity. The last century witnessed several views originating within the philosophy of science to demonstrate that scientific knowledge does not possess a superior status compared to other forms of knowledge. The methodology of science has been and continues to be subjected to extensive analysis and criticism in prominent ways to determine the standards by which scientific theories are measured and judged.

Several important thinkers have been involved in these analyses, beginning with Thomas Kuhn and including Karl Popper, Imre Lakatos, and Paul Feyerabend, to name a few.[1] The intriguing philosophical features of scientific methodology continue to be explored due to their useful traits in allowing us to sense that logical causality exists in statements made about the natural world.

Consider the following examples, one about astronomical phenomena and the other about human perspectives. They illustrate the differences that exist in our interpretation of their semantic richness, the differences between meanings:

I. The orbit of the planet Mars is an ellipse.
II. All planetary orbits are ellipses.

I. All misconceptions are preconceptions.
II. All preconceptions are misconceptions.

In the first example, the refutation or demonstration that statement I is false affects the truth of statement II, but not the other way around. In the second example, the refutation of either does not affect the other. Still, all these statements are based on experiences and observations, and they constitute items for analysis. But as stated, their truth or falsity is a logical function.

These rather simplistic examples are used to illustrate the perceived compelling power of logical—and, by extension, mathematical—statements made about the world. Therefore, despite the philosophical criticism that scientific theories have endured, they possess the powerful attraction of allowing us to think clearly.

The criticisms of the dogmatic aspects of scientific practice are relevant to our discussion of the metaphysical tendency to reject competing alternative hypotheses. The rather extreme view expressed by Feyerabend—completely rejecting the epistemic authority of science—can be seen as part of the denial that there is a single scientific method. More recently, other authors have argued that, despite there being a regular connection as part of our perception of causality in nature, regularity is not sufficient to justify the correctness of scientific laws.[2]

The assumption of causality seems to be supported by the results in experimental settings where one can see that there are links or associations between measured variables, particularly in epidemiological studies. Nevertheless, regularity fails to identify the *direction* of causality, even if it is determined to be present. As an example of this, consider the evidence that obesity is strongly linked to the incidence of diabetes. We can prevent the onset of the latter by implementing regimented weight control. However, if a cure were to be found for diabetes, this would not prevent obesity. In fact, it might even encourage its occurrence. The cure would no longer be merely prophylactic; it could very well be an *inducement*.

The modern difficulty in establishing a rationale for the existence of scientific laws may be due to the explicit exclusion of the Aristotelian "final" cause in scientific accounts of phenomena, as described in chapter 3. After this brief discussion of some of the issues surrounding the repeated attempts to find a justification for the existence of scientific theories and laws, we can attempt to provide a context where scientific knowledge can be seen from a wider perspective, that of flesh-and-blood human activity. This proposal is consistent with the views advocated by the great polymath and philosopher of science Michael Polanyi, particularly as expressed in his book *Personal Knowledge*.[3]

Our view of scientific knowledge as cumulative or progressively improving seems to be a fact of life in the modern world. However, can we say that every successive historical period has enjoyed more knowledge than its predecessors? Based on our discussion in previous chapters, we would have to admit that the Middle Ages represent an exception to this forward progression. A legitimate question, then, would be the likelihood that this backsliding would occur again in the future. That doesn't appear likely, given the recent and current frenetic pace of knowledge accumulation.

If science has enjoyed success due to the increasing fragmentation of knowledge that has led to the specialized modern scientific world, then we might see the recent claims that science is reaching an end in a new perspective. From an evolutionary viewpoint, overspecialization can lead to dead ends, particularly when drastic environmental changes occur. In terms of the evolution of ideas, the intellectual environment is similar to its biological counterpart. Only ideas that are *adaptive* can survive in a period of rapid change.

The integration of different forms of knowledge would seem necessary for a successful balance among the various needs of societies. A disproportionately scientific view of nature can hinder the development and establishment of a balanced view of the universe. Despite the many advantages offered by modern accomplishments in medicine, transportation, telecommunications, exploration, and other fields, human nature has remained essentially unchanged for much longer than science has been in existence.

The changes brought about through technological advances and the idea of progress have indeed transformed modern humans' outlook and the face of the planet. However, to declare that these changes have altered humanity's basic needs is naive. Among these needs are the spiritual ones and, as expressed by the Greek legacy, the beliefs that the universe is ordered and meaningful and that rationality provides the means to understand it. The latter are features of scientific knowledge, but not exclusively its province. Why should we expect, therefore, that science could possibly yield the answers to questions that it was never meant to address?

To clarify the last point, I must restate that the expectation that science can provide the answers to questions outside its domain is nothing new. There is a great example of an event relevant to this at the inception of the Royal Society of London, one of the earliest scientific organizations. (The story must remain anecdotal since I have been unable to confirm its scholarly origin other than to document where I encountered it.)[4]

According to this story, the English Crown requested the Royal Society to investigate a claim that a woman somewhere in the realm had given birth to a sheep. After all, although the general population could be counted on to believe such occurrences on account of their presumed ignorance, this would not be expected of the learned members of the realm at the Royal Society.

There are two points to consider about the event: First, if the Crown admitted the possibility of this being an actual occurrence of something clearly supernatural, then why not involve the organization most likely to deal with such matters—the Church? Second, since the Royal Society had a role as a scientific organization dedicated to investigating natural phenomena, why ask its members to settle a dispute concerning something that, from the perspective of the learned members of the realm, lies outside the order of nature?

The story about the Royal Society serves to illustrate that from the earliest stages of the existence of organized scientific knowledge, there has been a misplaced trust in its ability to solve even problems that, by their own nature, ought to lie outside the domain of science. It is also indicative of the confidence that society has continued to place on science to be the final judge on matters where it would be more appropriate to engage, enlist, or at the very least consult other organizations or social institutions. We must find a proper place for science in the larger context of human affairs. Otherwise, we risk continuing to misuse one of the greatest accomplishments in the history of our species.

Appendix A

Case I: Using a Force Sensor to Determine Specific Gravity

Legend says that Archimedes (c. 287–212 BC), one of the greatest mathematicians and inventors of all time, discovered the principle of displacement while stepping into a full bath. He realized that the water that ran over equaled in volume the submerged part of his body. The legend goes on to report that Archimedes was so excited by his discovery that he hopped out of the bath and rushed naked into the street, yelling triumphantly, "Eureka! Eureka!" ("I have found it!").

Another legend describes how Archimedes uncovered a fraud against King Hieron II of Syracuse using what has become known as his principle of buoyancy. The king suspected that a solid gold crown he ordered was partly made of silver. Archimedes conducted an experiment using two objects, one of pure gold and the other of pure silver, that had weights identical to the weight of the crown. He successively immersed the gold, the silver, and the crown in a container filled to the brim with water and measured the overflow of water, that is, the volume of water displaced by each material. He found that the crown displaced more water than the gold, but less than the silver, thereby proving that the crown contained some other metal that was less dense than gold. Figure A.1 shows how to conduct a similar experiment to determine the specific gravity or density of an object as Archimedes did.

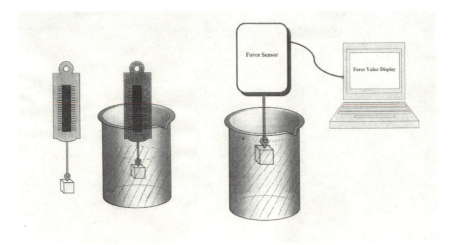

Using a Spring Balance   Using a Force Sensor

Figure A.1. Schematic of a demonstration of Archimedes' concept of buoyancy

Technique

1. Suspend the object from a spring balance and record the weight in newtons (N) in table A.1 below.
2. Immerse the same object in a container filled with water while still suspended from the spring balance. Make sure the object is completely submerged and doesn't touch the sides or bottom of the container. Record the spring balance reading.
3. Subtract the value in the water from the value in the air and enter the difference in the table.
4. Divide the value in the air by the difference (the value obtained in step 3) to determine the density of the object.
5. Repeat the above procedure using a force sensor instead of the spring balance. In each case, wait until the sensor reading stabilizes before recording the value in the table.

Using the equation for accuracy

$$\% \text{ error} = |\,(\text{standard value} - \text{experimental value}) / \text{standard value}\,| \times 100\% ,$$

compared with the standard density value of the object, how many times more accurate was the most reliable value determined?

Table A.1. Data for the Determination of the Specific Gravity/Density of an Object Using a Spring Balance and a Force Sensor

Object	Using Spring Balance				Using Force Sensor			
	Weight in air (W_a)	Weight in water (W_w)	Difference $W_a - W_w$ (Δ_{sb})	Density W_a / Δ_{sb}	Weight in air (W_a)	Weight in water (W_w)	Difference $W_a - W_w$ (Δ_{fs})	Density W_a / Δ_{fs}
(1)								
(2)								
(3)								
(4)								

Reflections

Discuss your results in terms of accuracy and sources of error that may account for your experimental findings.

Case II

One of the most important experiments in antiquity was that attributed to Eratosthenes (285–194 BCE), who used a simple technique to determine the circumference of the Earth. He realized that on the day of the summer solstice (June 21 or 22) a vertical object placed on the ground at Syene (modern Aswan) would cast no shadow at local noon (when the sun would be at the zenith). On the same day, an identical object *would* cast a shadow at local noon in Alexandria, as shown in figure A.2. By measuring the angle

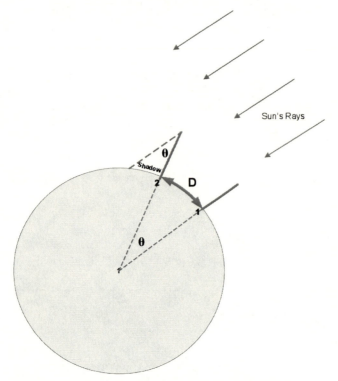

Figure A.2. Diagram illustrating that at Syene *(1)* there is no shadow cast by the vertical line at noon on the day of the summer solstice, whereas at Alexandria *(2)*, there is

subtended by the shadow, estimating the distance between the two locations, and using some geometric construction, Eratosthenes determined with considerable accuracy the Earth's circumference.

Procedure

Eratosthenes' method can be simulated in a darkened room, using a sphere made of material with two objects vertically inserted into, or fastened to, the surface, along with a light source at a distance sufficiently far to produce parallel rays striking the sphere.[1]

The first object is placed vertically at location (1); the second is then placed at (2), a distance D along a northern direction from the first. The sphere is then fastened to a surface or held steady so that, when the light source illuminates it, there will be no shadow projected at (1). The shadow length projected at (2) will then be measured, along with the length of the object at that location; additionally, the distance D between the two locations must be determined. A strip of paper can be used to measure both the length of the shadow and the distance between the locations; marks must be made on the paper so that accurate measurements can be obtained since the surface is curved. Two different trials are conducted, and their mean is used to compare with those obtained by other groups. The data are recorded in table A.2.

The calculations will be based on the quantities measured as illustrated in figure A.3. From the figure, we see that

$$\tan \theta = X/L$$

or

$$\theta = \arctan (X/L).$$

Table A.2. Individual Group Data and Results

Trial	Distance between Locations (D)	Length of Shadow (X)	Length of Object (L)	Angle (θ)	Circumference $C = 2\pi r$
1					
2					
Mean					

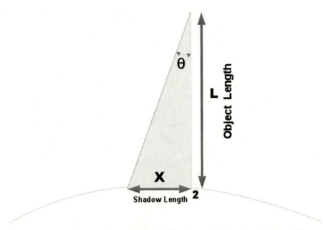

Figure A.3. **The angle subtended by the shadow is obtained from the measurements of the lengths of the shadow and the object.**

Since the entire circle contains 360°, the ratio of 360° to θ is the same as the ratio of the circumference C and the distance D between the two locations on the sphere; that is:

$$360°/\theta = C/D.$$

Solving for the circumference of the sphere, we get

$$C = (360°/\theta)\ D.$$

To relate our result from the sphere to the Earth, we need to determine the sphere's *scale*.

The ratio of the circumference to the entire circle is C/360°. Therefore dividing these numbers gives us a scale. To convert *n* centimeters to kilometers, multiply by the appropriate conversion:

$$(n\ \text{cm})\ (1\ \text{km}/10^5\ \text{cm}).$$

Since 1° of latitude on Earth represents a constant distance of 112 km, we can use as the Earth's scale 112 km = 1°, or 112 km/1°, and relate that to our sphere's scale.

_____ cm = 1° or
_____ cm / 1° → _____ km / 1°

We can compute the Earth's circumference by the following relationship:

Earth's circumference / sphere's circumference =
Earth's scale / sphere's scale.

If our measured sphere circumference is C (in km) and its scale is S km/1°, then we can substitute these known values:

$$C_{Earth}/C = (112 \text{ km}/1°) / (S \text{ km}/1°).$$

Solving for C_{Earth}, we get:

$$C_{Earth} = (112 \text{ km}/1°) (1°/S \text{ km}) (C).$$

This reduces to

$$C_{Earth} = (112/S)C.$$

To determine the accuracy and precision of the experiment, we need to tabulate the results from all the groups in table A.3.

- Accuracy:
- % Accuracy:
- % Precision:

Reflections
Record your reflections on the results (use accuracy, precision, and whatever you consider sources of error in the measurements as part of your comments).

Table A.3. Collective Determinations of Accuracy and Precision

Group	C_{Earth}	Uncertainty	Group	C_{Earth}	Uncertainty
1			7		
2			8		
3			9		
4			10		
5			11		
6			12		
Mean					Precision

Questions
1. Why is the experiment on Earth likely to yield reliable results only if at least one location has a latitude value smaller than 23.5° either north or south?
2. Why must the two objects be aligned roughly north or south?

Case III

Attempts to understand the way objects fall to the ground have been numerous and extensively documented. One of the earliest correct explanations was provided by a successor of Aristotle, Strato (c. 335–269 BCE). He observed, as anyone clearly can, that water falling from a spout breaks up before hitting the ground. He concluded that since the water starts falling continuously and then breaks up, it must be that the water at the bottom of the breaking portion is moving faster than that at the top. This is essentially what Galileo later discovered applies to all falling objects. In modern terms, the water breaks up because it doesn't move with a constant speed; instead, it is accelerating as it falls.

Determination of the Local Gravitational Acceleration (g) by Dropping Objects from a Height
The situation is shown in figure A.4.
    The equation that describes the fall of an object from rest is obtained from

$$S = S_i + v_i t + (1/2)at^2,$$

where:

S_i is an initial position that can be taken to be zero as a point of reference;
v_i is the initial velocity, which can be taken to be zero if the object is released at the same instant that the time begins to be measured;
a is acceleration; and
t is time elapsed.

This equation reduces to

$$H = (1/2)gt^2,$$

where:

H is the height;
g is the acceleration of gravity; and
t is the time of fall.

Figure A.4. Cartoon illustrating a person dropping an object from a building while someone else is clocking the motion to determine how long it takes to hit the ground

Solving for g, we get:

$$g = 2H/t^2.$$

Conduct your own trials of this experiment. Input the data in table A.4. The standard value of g is 980.3 cm/sec^2.

Table A.4. Data for the Various Height and Time Measurements.

Height (H) in m	Time (t) in sec	Time²	g (cm/sec²)	% Error

- Average value of g = _____ cm/sec²
- Average % error =

Comment on the results of your own group and how these compare to the class average, and the sources of error in this experiment.

Determination of g Using a Simple Pendulum

As shown in figure 8.1 earlier, in this activity we'll use a simple pendulum to determine the local acceleration of gravity (g) on the Earth.

Vary the length of the pendulum, and for each value determine the period by using the photo-gate as the time-measuring device; take three different readings of the period for each length, and then enter the average value in table A.5. Fill in the values for the period squared as well.

Graph the period squared as a function of the pendulum length in figure A.5.

Table A.5. Data for the Period and the Period Squared of the Pendulum

Length [L] (cm)	Period [T] (sec)	Period Squared [T²] (sec²)

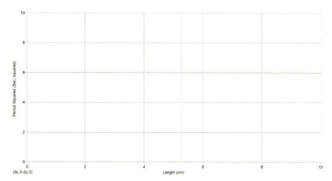

Figure A.5. Plot of the period squared as a function of the length of the pendulum

$$T = 2\pi \sqrt{\frac{L}{g}} \tag{1}$$

$$T^2 = 4\pi^2 L/g = (4\pi^2/g)\, L \tag{2}$$

This is the equation describing the relationship between the variables in figure A.5; it is of the form

$$y = mx + b, \tag{3}$$

where m is the slope. And the slope from (2) is $4\pi^2/g$. Hence,

$$\underline{\hspace{3cm}} \text{ sec}^2/\text{cm} = 4\pi^2/g.$$

Solving for g:

$$g = 4\pi^2/\,\underline{\hspace{2cm}}\, \text{sec}^2/\text{cm}.$$

Substituting the values, we get:

$$g = (4)\,(3.14)^2/.\underline{\hspace{2cm}}\, \text{sec}^2/\text{ cm} = \underline{\hspace{2cm}}\text{cm/sec}^2.$$

The percentage error is found using the following equation:

$$\% \text{ error} = |\,(980.3 \text{ cm/sec}^2 - \underline{\hspace{2cm}} \text{ cm/sec}^2)\,/$$
$$980.3 \text{ cm/sec}^2\,| \times 100\%$$

Reflect on the sources of error that could have contributed to your experimental result.

~

Appendix B

This appendix describes an experiment similar to the one discussed in chapter 8. Data are shown in table B.1.

The experimentally determined period is

$$T_{exp.} = 1.618395 \pm .000180 \text{ sec}$$

with a precision equal to the average uncertainty, that is:

$$\text{Precision} = \sum(\text{Uncertainties}) / 30 = .000180 \text{ sec.}$$

The theoretical period T_{th} (that predicted by the equation describing simple harmonic motion of a pendulum) is:

$$T_{th} = 2\pi \sqrt{\frac{l}{g}} ,$$

where:

$g = 980.3 \text{ cm/sec}^2$; and
l = length of the pendulum.

Table B.1. Determination of the Experimental Period for a Simple Pendulum of Length 65 cm When the Angle of Oscillation Is about 5 Degrees

Trial	Period	Uncertainty [|Period – Average|]
1	1.618390	.000005
2	1.618341	.000054
3	1.618414	.000019
4	1.618458	.000063
5	1.618429	.000034
6	1.618601	.000206
7	1.618684	.000289
8	1.618545	.000150
9	1.618602	.000207
10	1.618602	.000207
11	1.618806	.000411
12	1.618603	.000208
13	1.618401	.000006
14	1.617901	.000494
15	1.618236	.000159
16	1.618100	.000295
17	1.618301	.000094
18	1.618104	.000291
19	1.618274	.000121
20	1.618101	.000294
Average	**1.618395**	**.000180**

Therefore,

$$T_{th} = 2\,(3.1416)\,(65.0 \text{ cm} / 980.3 \text{ cm/sec}^2)^{1/2}$$

$$T_{th} = 1.617848 \text{ sec.}$$

The accuracy and percentage of precision and accuracy are calculated as follows:

$$\text{Accuracy} = (\text{Average } T_{exp}) - T_{th}$$

$$= 1.618395 \text{ sec} - 1.617848 \text{ sec} = .000547 \text{ sec}$$

$$\% \text{ Precision} = [\text{Precision} / \text{Average}] \times 100\%$$

$$= .000180 \text{ sec} / 1.618395 \times 100\% = .011\%$$

% Accuracy = | (Theoretical Period – Experimental Period)/
Theoretical Period | × 100%

$$= | (T_{th} - T_{exp})/T_{th} | \times 100\%$$

$$= | (1.617848 \text{ sec} - 1.618395 \text{ sec})/1.617848 \text{ sec} | \times 100\%$$

$$= .033\%$$

Finally, the ratio of the two percentages, % Accuracy to % Precision, is

$$.033\%/.011\% = 3.07,$$

meaning that the result is about three times more precise than accurate. The graphs are shown in figure B.1.

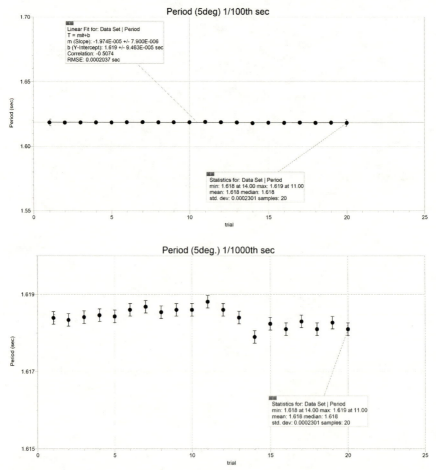

Figure B.1. Graphs of the period when plotted at the 1/100th of a second and the 1/1000th of a second sensitivity

~

Notes

Preface

1. C. Mooney and S. Kirshenbaum, *Unscientific America: How Scientific Illiteracy Threatens Our Future* (New York: Basic Books, 2009).

2. R. W. Hazen and J. Trefil, *Science Matters: Achieving Scientific Literacy* (New York: Anchor Books, 1992).

Introduction

1. K. C. Stange, "Ways of Knowing, Learning, and Developing," *Annals of Family Medicine* 8, no. 1 (January/February 2010): 4–10.

2. D. Kolb, *Experiential Learning: Experience as the Source of Learning and Development* (Englewood Cliffs, NJ: Prentice-Hall, 1984).

Chapter 1: The Need for Scientific Literacy

1. J. Carey, "Putting the Weirdness to Work," *Business Week*, March 15, 2004, 103–5.

2. The work of Dr. Jon Miller is particularly noteworthy; see "Scientific Savvy? In U.S. Not Much," *New York Times*, August 30, 2005.

3. N. Rosenberg and L. E. Birdzell, "Science, Technology and the Western Miracle," *Scientific American* 263, no. 5 (1990): 42–54.

4. M. Gibbons, "Science's New Social Contract with Society," *Nature* 402, no. 6761 supp. (1999): C81–C84.

5. T. Roszak, *Where the Wasteland Ends: Politics and Transcendence in Post-industrial Society* (New York: Doubleday Anchor Books, 1973).

6. A. J. Petto and L. R. Godfrey, eds., *Scientists Confront Creationism: Intelligent Design and Beyond* (New York: Norton, 2008).

7. "*Kitzmiller v. Dover Area School District*, Trial Transcript: Day 3 (September 28), AM Session, Part 1," *TalkOrigins Archive*, http://www.talkorigins.org/faqs/dover/day3am.html.

8. K. R. Popper, *Conjectures and Refutations: The Growth of Scientific Knowledge* (London: Routledge, 1992), 216.

9. J. Bennett, E. Donahue, N. Schneider, and M. Voit, *The Essential Cosmic Perspective*, 4th ed. (San Francisco: Pearson/Addison-Wesley, 2006), 75.

10. S. Cole, "The Hierarchy of the Sciences?" *American Journal of Sociology* 89, no. 1 (1983): 111–39.

11. D. Fanelli, "'Positive' Results Increase down the Hierarchy of the Sciences," *PLoS One* 5, no. 4 (2010), http://www.plosone.org/article/info:doi%2F10.1371%2Fjournal.pone.0010068.

12. Royal Society, "History," http://royalsociety.org/about-us/history/.

13. P. Duhem, *Essays in the History and Philosophy of Science*, trans. R. Ariew and P. Barker (Indianapolis: Hackett, 1954).

14. P. Medawar, *The Threat and the Glory: Reflections on Science and Scientists* (New York: HarperCollins, 1990), 12.

Chapter 2: The Origins of Accomplishing Tasks

1. N. Toth, "The First Technology," *Scientific American* 256, no. 4 (1987): 112–22.

2. O. T. Mason, *The Origins of Invention* (London: W. Scott Ltd., 1895).

3. E. A. Speiser, "Ancient Mesopotamia and the Beginnings of Science," in University of Pennsylvania, Bicentennial Conference, *Studies in the History of Science* (Philadelphia: University of Pennsylvania Press, 1941), 1–11.

4. A. Gillaume, *Prophecy and Divination among the Hebrews and Other Semites* (New York: Harper, 1938).

5. F. Thureau-Dangin, "History of the Sexagesimal System," *Osiris* 7 (1939): 95–141.

6. S. R. K. Glanville, ed., *The Legacy of Egypt* (Oxford: Clarendon Press, 1942).

7. J. H. Breasted, *The Edwin Smith Surgical Papyrus, Published in Facsimile and Hyeroglyphic Transliteration with Translation and Commentary*, 2 vols. (Chicago: University of Chicago Press, 1930).

8. H. H. Sigerist, *A History of Medicine*, vol. 1: *Primitive and Archaic Medicine* (New York: Oxford University Press, 1951).

9. J. Needham, *Science and Civilisation in China*, 7 vols. (Cambridge: Cambridge University Press, 1954).

Chapter 3: The Earliest Comprehensive and Rationalistic Syntheses

1. J. St. B. T. Evans, "Dual-Processing Accounts of Reasoning, Judgment, and Social Cognition," *Annual Review of Psychology* 59 (2008): 255–78.

2. R. S. Nickerson, "Confirmation Bias: A Ubiquitous Phenomenon in Many Guises," *Review of General Psychology* 2, no. 2 (1998): 175–220.

3. H. H. Titus, *Living Issues in Philosophy*, 5th ed. (New York: Van Nostrand, 1964); E. L. Gettier, *"Is Justified True Belief* Knowledge?" *Analysis* 23 (1963), 121–23; T. Williamson, *Knowledge and Its Limits* (Oxford: Oxford University Press, 2002.

4. G. S. Kirk and J. E. Raven, *The Presocratic Philosophers: A Critical History with a Selection of Texts* (Cambridge: Cambridge University Press, 1960).

5. C. H. Kahn, *Anaximander and the Origins of Greek Cosmology* (New York: Columbia University Press, 1960); D. Furley, *Cosmic Problems: Essays on Greek and Roman Philosophy of Nature* (Cambridge: Cambridge University Press, 1989).

6. D. Furley, *The Greek Cosmologists*, vol. 1, *The Formation of the Atomic Theory and Its Earliest Critics* (Cambridge: Cambridge University Press, 1987).

7. Plato, *Republic*, trans. Francis M. Cornford (Oxford: Oxford University Press, 1941).

8. G. Vlastos, *Plato's Universe* (Seattle: University of Washington Press, 1975).

9. G. E. R. Lloyd, *Aristotle: The Growth and Structure of His Thought* (Cambridge: Cambridge University Press, 1968).

10. G. E. R. Lloyd, *Magic, Reason and Experience: Studies in the Origins and Development of Greek Science* (Cambridge: Cambridge University Press, 1979).

11. Plato, *Plato's Theory of Knowledge: The "Theaetetus" and the "Sophist" of Plato*, trans. with commentary by F. M. Cornford (1935; reprint, Oxford: Oxford University Press, 2001).

12. A. Edel, *Aristotle and His Philosophy* (Chapel Hill: University of North Carolina Press, 1982).

13. J. Barnes, "Aristotle's Theory of Demonstration," in J. Barnes, M. Schofield, and R. Sorabji, *Articles on Aristotle*, vol. 1, *Science* (London: Duckworth, 1975), 65–87.

14. J. A. Weisheipl, *The Development of Physical Theory in the Middle Ages* (New York: Sheed & Ward, 1959).

15. F. Espinoza, "An Analysis of the Historical Development of Ideas about Motion and Its Implications for Teaching," *Physics Education* 40, no. 2 (2005): 139–46.

16. M. Clagett, *The Science of Mechanics in the Middle Ages* (Madison: University of Wisconsin Press, 1959).

17. D. Bohm, *Wholeness and the Implicate Order* (London: Routledge & Kegan Paul, 1980).

18. Aristotle, *The Complete Works*, ed. J. Barnes, 2 vols. (Princeton, NJ: Princeton University Press, 1912).

19. *The Works of Archimedes: Edited in Modern Notation, with Introductory Chapters*, ed. T. L. Heath, 2nd ed. (Cambridge: Cambridge University Press, 1912; reprint, Mineola, NY: Dover, 2002).

Chapter 4: Knowing, Doing, and the Inevitability of Curiosity and Exploration

1. W. H. Stahl, *Roman Science: Origins, Development and Influence to the Later Middle Ages* (Madison: University of Wisconsin Press, 1962).

2. S. Bramly, *Leonardo: The Artist and the Man* (New York: Penguin Books, 1998), 206.

3. F. S. Merritt, *Building Design and Construction Handbook*, 4th ed. (New York: McGraw-Hill, 1982), sec. 4-20, table 4-10.

4. G. Hauck, "The Roman Aqueduct of Nimes," *Scientific American* 260, no. 3 (1989): 98–104.

5. E. Rawson, *Intellectual Life in the Late Roman Republic* (Baltimore: Johns Hopkins University Press, 1985).

6. D. C. Lindberg, *The Beginnings of Western Science* (Chicago: University of Chicago Press, 1992).

7. D. C. Lindberg, "Alhazen's Theory of Vision and Its Reception in the West," *Isis* 58 (1967): 321–41.

8. D. G. Pelli, "Close Encounters: An Artist Shows That Size Affects Shape," *Science* 285 (1999): 844–46.

9. C. Singer, *A Short History of Anatomy and Physiology from the Greeks to Harvey* (New York: Dover, 1957).

10. L. Garcia Ballester, "Galen as a Medical Practitioner: Problems in Diagnosis," in *Galen: Problems and Prospects*, ed. V. Nutton (London: Wellcome Institute for the History of Medicine, 1981), 13–46.

11. D. J. Boorstin, *The Discoverers: A History of Man's Search to Know His World and Himself* (New York: Vintage Books, 1985).

Chapter 5: From the Transcendent to the Temporal

1. J. Burke, *The Day the Universe Changed* (Boston: Little, Brown, 1997).

2. J. Marenbon, *The Philosophy of Peter Abelard* (Cambridge: Cambridge University Press, 1997); E. Voegelin, "Siger De Bravant," *Philosophy and Phenomenological Research* 4, no. 4 (1944): 507–26.

3. R. B. Burke, *The Opus Majus of Roger Bacon*, 2 vols. (Philadelphia: University of Pennsylvania Press, 1928; reprint, New York: Kessinger, 2002).

4. R. Taylor, *Metaphysics* (Englewood Cliffs, NJ: Prentice-Hall, 1974), 98.

5. *Opera Omnia* ("The Vatican Edition"), *Civitas Vaticana: Typis Polyglottis Vaticanis*, 1950–. Ordinatio, book 2 (vols. 1–7).

6. D. C. Baird, *Experimentation: An Introduction to Measurement Theory and Experimental Design* (Englewood Cliffs, NJ: Prentice-Hall, 1962), 6.

7. D. Bohm, *Causality and Chance in Modern Physics* (New York: Harper & Brothers, 1961), 10.

8. R. Feynman, *The Character of Physical Law* (Cambridge, MA: MIT Press, 1989), 54–55.

9. C. L. Smith and L. Wenk, "Relations among Three Aspects of First-Year College Students' Epistemologies of Science," *Journal of Research in Science Teaching* 43, no. 8 (2006): 747–85.

Chapter 6: From Qualities to Quantities

1. Archimedes, *Archimedes in the Middle Ages*, ed. and trans. M. Clagett, 5 vols. (Madison: University of Wisconsin Press, 1964).

2. E. J. Dijksterhuis, *Archimedes*, trans. C. Dikshoorn (Copenhagen: Munksgaard, 1956); E. J. Dijksterhuis, *The Mechanization of the World Picture*, trans. C. Dikshoorn (Oxford: Clarendon Press, 1961).

3. W. A. Wallace, "The 'Calculatores' in Early Sixteenth-Century Physics," *British Journal for the History of Science* 10, no. 3 (1969): 221–32.

4. C. C. Gillispie, *The Edge of Objectivity* (Princeton, NJ: Princeton University Press, 1990), 41.

5. C. P. Snow, *The Two Cultures and the Scientific Revolution* (New York: Cambridge University Press, 1963; reprint, 1993).

6. E. M. Klaaren, *Religious Origins of Modern Science* (Grand Rapids, MI: Eerdmans, 1977).

7. F. Bacon, *New Organon*, ed. L. Jardine and M. Silverthone (Cambridge: Cambridge University Press, 2000).

8. D. Hume, *Enquiry concerning Human Understanding*. London, 1748. Modern ed. by Tom L. Beauchamp (Oxford: Oxford University Press, 1999).

9. S. Weinberg, "Can Science Explain Everything? Anything?" *New York Review of Books*, May 31, 2001, 47–50.

10. M. Gu et al., "More Really Is Different," *Physica D: Nonlinear Phenomena* 238 (2009): 835.

Chapter 7: Internalizing Naturalistic Explanations

1. J. Monod, *Chance and Necessity* (New York: Knopf, 1971).

2. G. S. Stent, *Paradoxes of Progress* (San Francisco: W. H. Freeman, 1978).

3. E. Mayr, "Teleological and Teleonomic: A New Analysis," *Boston Studies in the Philosophy of Science* 14 (1974): 91–117.

4. N. R. Hanson, *Patterns of Discovery* (Cambridge: Cambridge University Press, 1958).

5. S. Schweber, "The Origin of the Origin Revisited," *Journal of the History of Biology* 10 (1977): 229–316.

6. C. H. Waddington, *The Evolution of an Evolutionist* (Edinburgh: Edinburgh University Press, 1975); P. Weiss, "The Living System: Determinism Stratified," in *Beyond Reductionism*, ed. A. Koestler and J. R. Smythies, 3–55 (London: Hutchinson, 1969).

7. I. Prigogine and I. Stengers, *Order Out of Chaos* (Toronto: Bantam Books, 1984).

8. E. O. Wilson, *On Human Nature* (Cambridge, MA: Harvard University Press, 1978).

9. K. Miller, *Finding Darwin's God: A Scientist's Search for Common Ground between God and Evolution* (New York: HarperCollins, 1999), 186.

10. R. Lewontin, "Billions and Billions of Demons," *New York Review of Books*, January 9, 1997, 31.

11. J. A. Coyne, "Seeing and Believing: The Never-Ending Attempt to Reconcile Science and Religion, and Why It Is Doomed to Fail," *New Republic*, February 4, 2009.

12. T. Eagleton, *Reason, Faith, and Revolution: Reflections on the God Debate* (New Haven, CT: Yale University Press, 2009), 145.

13. M. Midgley, "Can Science Save Its Soul?" *New Scientist*, August 1, 1992, 24–27.

Chapter 8: Dispensing with Philosophy and Entertaining Limits to Human Knowledge

1. N. Oreskes, K. Shrader-Frechette, and K. Belitz, "Verification, Validation, and Confirmation of Numerical Models in the Earth Sciences," *Science* 263, no. 4 (1994): 641–46.

2. E. Nagel and J. R. Newman, *Godel's Proof* (New York: New York University Press, 1958).

3. S. Schiffer, "Ceteris Paribus Laws," *Mind* 100 (1991): 397–414.

4. K. Popper, *The Logic of Scientific Discovery* (London: Hyman, 1959).

5. T. Kuhn, *The Structure of Scientific Revolutions* (Chicago: University of Chicago Press, 1970).

6. G. Fowles, *Analytical Mechanics* (New York: Holt, Rinehart & Winston, 1970), 101–2.

7. M. Boas, *Mathematical Methods in the Physical Sciences* (New York: John Wiley & Sons, 1983), 403.

8. R. Penrose, "What Is Reality?" *New Scientist*, November 18, 2006, 32.

9. P. Schilpp, ed., *Albert Einstein: Philosopher-Scientist* (New York: Tudor, 1949).

10. A. E. Lawson, "Basic Inferences of Scientific Reasoning, Argumentation, and Discovery," *Science Education* 94, no. 2 (2010): 336–64.

Chapter 9: Scientifically Speaking, We Know a Lot—or Do We?

1. G. Holton, *Science and Anti-Science* (Cambridge, MA: Harvard University Press, 1993), 137.

2. E. Mach, *The Science of Mechanics*, 3rd paperback ed. (LaSalle, IL: Open Court Press, 1974), 161.

3. L. Thomas, "The Art of Teaching Science," *New York Times Magazine*, March 14, 1982.

4. D. Schneck, "Perceived Reality: Hidden Variables," *American Laboratory*, March 2004, 4–6, and private correspondence.

5. J. Horgan, "From Complexity to Perplexity," *Scientific American* 272, no. 6 (1995): 104–9.

6. J. M. Smith, "The Limitations of Evolution Theory," in *The Encyclopedia of Ignorance*, ed. R. Duncan and M. Weston-Smith (Oxford: Pergamon Press, 1977), 235–42; J. W. Drake, "The Role of Mutation in Microbial Evolution," *Symposium of the Society for General Microbiology* 24 (1974): 41–58.

7. M. A. Nowak and K. Sigmund, "Evolution of Indirect Reciprocity," *Nature* 437, no. 27 (2005): 1291–98.

8. E. Jablonka and M. J. Lamb, *Epigenetic Inheritance and Evolution: The Lamarckian Dimension* (Oxford: Oxford University Press, 1995).

9. M. Foucault, *The Archeology of Knowledge*, Engl. trans. ed. (London: Tavistock, 1972); J. Dupre, *The Disorder of Things: Metaphysical Foundations of the Disunity of Life* (Cambridge, MA: Harvard University Press, 1993).

10. D. Chalmers, *The Conscious Mind: In Search of a Fundamental Theory* (New York: Oxford University Press, 1996).

11. H. Atmanspacher, "Quantum Theory and Consciousness: An Overview of Selected Examples," *Discrete Dynamics in Nature and Society* 8 (2004): 51–73.

12. R. Penrose, *The Emperor's New Mind* (Oxford: Oxford University Press, 1989); R. Penrose, *Shadows of the Mind* (Oxford: Oxford University Press, 1994).

13. E. Wigner, "The Unreasonable Effectiveness of Mathematics in the Natural Sciences," *Communications in Pure and Applied Mathematics* 13, no. 1 (1960).

14. M. Tegmark, "The Mathematical Universe," *Foundations of Physics* 38, no. 2 (2007): 101–50.

15. L. Wolpert, *The Unnatural Nature of Science* (London: Faber & Faber, 1992).

16. J. Ziman, "Pushing Back Frontiers—or Redrawing Maps!" in *The Identification of Progress in Learning*, ed. T. Hägerstrand (Cambridge: Cambridge University Press, 1985), 1–12.

Chapter 10: The Need for a Context

1. A. Funkenstein, *Theology and the Scientific Imagination from the Middle Ages to the Seventeenth Century* (Princeton, NJ: Princeton University Press, 1986), 117–201; E. Serene, "Demonstrative Science," in *The Cambridge History of Later Medieval Philosophy*, ed. N. Kretzmann, A. Kenny, and J. Pinborg (Cambridge: Cambridge University Press, 1982), 496–517.

2. J. A. Wheeler, "Information, Physics, Quantum: The Search for Links," in *Complexity, Entropy and the Physics of Information*, ed. W. Zurek (Redwood City, CA: Addison-Wesley, 1990), 3; B. Greene, *The Elegant Universe: Superstrings, Hidden Dimensions, and the Quest for the Ultimate Theory* (New York: Vintage Books, 2000).

3. G. E. Christianson, *In the Presence of the Creator: Isaac Newton and His Times* (New York: Free Press, 1984).

4. R. S. Westfall, "Newton and the Fudge Factor," *Science* 179, no. 4075 (1973): 751–58.

5. M. Ruse, "Darwin's Debt to Philosophy," *Studies in History and Philosophy of Science* 6 (1975): 159–81.

6. C. Kenneally, "Evolution without Natural Selection," *New Scientist*, September 2008, 40–43.

7. L. Schiff, *Quantum Mechanics*, 3rd ed. (New York: McGraw-Hill, 1968).

8. K. R. Popper, *Quantum Theory and the Schism in Physics* (Totowa, NJ: Rowman & Littlefield, 1982).

9. C. Kiefer, "On the Interpretation of Quantum Theory: From Copenhagen to the Present Day," arXiv:quant-ph/0210152v1, 2002.

10. M. Born, *Natural Philosophy of Cause and Chance* (Oxford: Clarendon Press, 1949).

11. Popper, *Quantum Theory*, 105–15.

12. P. M. Lee, *Bayesian Statistics: An Introduction* (Oxford: Oxford University Press, 1989).

13. R. T. Cox, "Probability, Frequency and Reasonable Expectation," *American Journal of Physics* 14, no. 1 (1946): 1–13.

14. W. Heitler, "The Departure from Classical Thought in Modern Physics," in *Albert Einstein: Philosopher-Scientist*, ed. P. A. Schilpp (New York: Tudor, 1949), 194ff.

15. W. Heisenberg, "The Development of the Interpretation of the Quantum Theory," in *Niels Bohr and the Development of Physics*, ed. W. Pauli (London: Pergamon Press), 12–29.

16. As quoted in M. J. Wheatley, *Leadership and the New Science: Discovering Order in a Chaotic World*, 2nd ed. (San Francisco: Berrett-Koehler, 1999), 32.

17. K. R. Popper, *Realism and the Aim of Science*, ed. W. W. Bartley III (London: Hutchinson, 1983).

18. B. Rosenblum and F. Kuttner, *Quantum Enigma: Physics Encounters Consciousness* (Oxford: Oxford University Press, 2006).

19. J. D. Barrow and F. J. Tipler, *The Anthropic Cosmological Principle* (Oxford: Oxford University Press, 1985).

20. B. S. DeWitt and N. Graham, eds., *The Many-Worlds Interpretation of Quantum Mechanics* (Princeton, NJ: Princeton University Press, 1973).

21. F. J. Tipler, "The Many-Worlds Interpretation of Quantum Mechanics in Quantum Cosmology," in *Quantum Concepts in Space and Time*, ed. R. Penrose and C. J. Isham (Oxford: Clarendon Press, 1986), 204–14.

22. W. Sandoval, "Conceptual and Epistemic Aspects of Students' Scientific Explanations," *Journal of the Learning Sciences* 12 (2003): 5–51.

23. R. Bybee, B. McCrae, and R. Laurie, "PISA 2006: An Assessment of Scientific Literacy," *Journal of Research in Science Teaching* 46, no. 8 (2009): 865–83.

Chapter 11: The Rightful Place of Science in Society

1. A report based on work at the International University of Paris can be found at www.templeton.org/newsroom/Intelligent_Design/Collective_Article.pdf.

2. N. Maxwell, "The Need for a Revolution in the Philosophy of Science," *Journal for General Philosophy of Science* 33 (2002): 381–408.

3. N. Maxwell, "Can Humanity Learn to Become Civilized? The Crisis of Science without Civilization," *Journal of Applied Philosophy* 17, no. 1 (2000): 29–44.

4. J. Ziman, "Is Science Losing Its Objectivity?" *Nature* 382 (1996): 751–54.

5. N. L. Kerr, "HARKing: Hypothesizing After the Results are Known," *Personality and Social Psychology Review* 2, no. 3 (1998): 196–217.

6. D. Mayo, *Error and the Growth of Experimental Knowledge* (Chicago: University of Chicago Press, 1996); D. Mayo, "Duhem's Problem, the Bayesian Way, and Error Statistics: What's Belief Got to Do with It?" *Philosophy of Science* 64 (1997): 222–44.

7. N. Maxwell, *Is Science Neurotic?* (London: Imperial College Press, 2004).

8. B. Latour and S. Woolgar, *Laboratory Life: The Social Construction of Scientific Facts* (Beverly Hills, CA: Sage, 1979).

9. H. M. Collins, "Son of Seven Sexes: The Social Destruction of a Physical Phenomenon," *Social Studies of Science* 11 (1981): 33–62.

10. R. Shorto, *Descartes' Bones: A Skeletal History of the Conflict between Faith and Reason* (New York: Vintage Books, 2008).

11. See http://www.aaas.org/spp/dser/.

12. J. Knobe, "The New Science of Morality, Part 8," presentation, September 17, 2010, http://edge.org/conversation/the-new-science-of-morality-part-8.

13. National Research Council, *National Science Education Standards* (Washington, DC: National Academy Press, 1996).

14. National Research Council, *Inquiry and the National Science Education Standards: A Guide for Teaching and Learning* (Washington, DC: National Academy Press, 2000).

15. B. A. Wallace, *The Taboo of Subjectivity* (New York: Oxford University Press, 2000).

16. E. Boutroux, *Science and Religion in Contemporary Philosophy*, trans. J. Nield (New York: Macmillan, 1911).

17. W. James, "The Notion of Consciousness," in *The Writings of William James*, ed. J. J. McDermott (1905; reprint, Chicago: University of Chicago Press, 1977), 184–94; E. Squires, "Quantum Theory and the Need for Consciousness," *Journal of Consciousness Studies* 1, no. 2 (1994): 201–4; H. Stapp, *Mind, Matter and Quantum Mechanics* (Berlin: Springer-Verlag, 1993).

18. J. Searle, *The Rediscovery of the Mind* (Cambridge, MA: MIT Press, 1994).

19. K. Prewitt, "Scientific Illiteracy and Democratic Theory," *Daedalus* 112, no. 2 (1983): 60.

Chapter 12: Concluding Reflections

1. I. Lakatos and A. Musgrave, eds., *Criticism and the Growth of Knowledge* (Cambridge: Cambridge University Press, 1970).

2. A. F. Chalmers, *What Is This Thing Called Science?*, 3rd ed. (Indianapolis: Hackett, 1999).

3. M. Polanyi, *Personal Knowledge: Towards a Post-Critical Philosophy* (Chicago: University of Chicago Press, 1958).

4. D. Robinson, *Great Ideas in Philosophy*, 2nd ed., Course no. 4206, Teaching Company.

Appendix A

1. F. Espinoza, "Measuring the Size of the Earth," in *Astronomy 98/99*, ed. D. Dathe (Guilford, CT: Dushkin/McGraw-Hill, 1998), 52.

Index

~

About the Author

Fernando Espinoza holds a joint appointment as associate professor in the Department of Chemistry and Physics and in the School of Education at the State University of New York College at Old Westbury. He also holds a part-time faculty appointment in the Department of Physics and Astronomy at Hofstra University. He received his doctorate from Columbia University, where he studied and did research in physics education, with an emphasis on the pedagogical implications of the cognitive aspects of learning mechanics. At Old Westbury, Dr. Espinoza directs the graduate programs in education, and coordinates the undergraduate and graduate science education program. He teaches graduate courses on the nature and development of science, upon which this book is based, on topics in Earth and space science, and on methods of teaching science. At Hofstra, he teaches a course on the physics of sound, as well as undergraduate and graduate astronomy courses.

Dr. Espinoza is the author of more than a dozen peer-reviewed publications in physics education and science education, as well as a number of other scholarly works at the national and international level. He is an accomplished winemaker and lives in Northport, Long Island, with his wife Katherine and their four children, Victoria, Gabriella, Gerard, and Olivia.